The Wisdom of Kashmir Shaivism

Revealed by
His Holiness,

Swami Lakshmanjoo

WITH ORIGINAL AUDIO/VIDEO

Viresh Hughes, Editor

Lakshmanjoo Academy

Published by Lakshmanjoo Academy

First printing 2024

Printed in the United States of America

For information, address:
Lakshmanjoo Academy
www.lakshmanjooacademy.org

ISBN 978-1-947241-22-0 (hardcover)
ISBN 978-1-947241-21-3 (paperback)
ISBN 978-1-947241-23-7 (ebook)

This sacred text is dedicated to Swami Lakshmanjoo,
our beloved teacher and spiritual father
who has given us everything.
Glory be to Thee!

Table of Contents

Guide to Pronunciation vii
Introduction viii
Acknowledgments xi
Swami Lakshmanjoo xv

The Wisdom of Kashmir Shaivism

Verse Page

01-10 Meditation 1
11 Avasthā Bheda Prakriyā 11
The Paths of the States (of Consciousness)
12 Pramātṛ Bheda Prakriyā 12
The Paths of Subjectivity
13 Kṛtya Bheda Prakriyā 13
The Paths of Action
14 Dvādaśakalīnāṁ Prādubhāvasthitiḥ 14
The Rise of the Twelve Kālīs
15 Adhva Bheda Prakriyā 16
The Paths of the Orbits
16-21 Śaktipātasya Vaicitryam 19
The Variations of Grace
22-24 Samadhānaṁ Vinā Śāstrāṇaṁ Vaiyarthyam 24
Scriptures Are Useless Without Practice
25-27 Kadā Guruḥ Śiṣyahṛdayajjñānāharaṇaṁ Kuryat 27
When a Master Should Extract a Disciple's Spiritual Knowledge
28-29 Patiśivaśabdayoḥ Nirvacanam 32
Nominating Śiva as "Pati"
30 Mahābhairavadeva Śabdasya Nirvacanam 34
The Explanation of "Mahābhairava Deva"
31-42 Bhairava Śabdasya Nirvacanam 35
The Explanation of "Bhairava"
43-47 Utkrānti Vidhi Kramaḥ 49
The Master's Procedure for a Dying Disciple
48-58 Yogasya Mahatvam (Bhagavad Gītā) 56
The Essence of Yoga

59-72 Mokṣasya Lakṣanam 75
The Definition of "Liberation"
73-85 Srīrāmaśabdasya Pāramārthikatvam 96
The Reality of the Word "Rama"
86-88 Vastutaḥ Śivasyaiva Sarvabhāvena Kartṛtvam 112
Everything is Done By Lord Śiva
89 Mahākālī 115

Appendix

1. Wisdom of Kashmir Shaivism 119
Verses Only for Recitation
2. Krama Stotra 140
Hymn to the Twelve Kālīs
3. Anuttarāṣṭikā of Abhinavagupta 149
Eight Verses on the Supreme (Anuttara)
4. Bhairava Stotra of Abhinavagupta 154
Hymn to Bhairava
5. Dehasthadevatācakra Stotra of Abhinavagupta 158
Hymn to the Gods and Goddesses Residing in One's Own Body
6. Sixteen Amṛtas (Nectars) 164

Bibliography 170
Index 172
Instructions to download audio 181

Guide to Pronunciation

The following English words exemplify the pronunciation of selected Sanskrit vowels and consonants. The Romanized Sanskrit vowel or consonant is first listed and then an English word is given to aid you in its proper pronunciation.

a	as	a in ***A***merica.
ā	as	a in f***a***ther.
i	as	i in f***i***ll, l***i***ly.
ī	as	i in pol***i***ce.
u	as	u in f***u***ll.
ū	as	u in r***u***de.
ṛ	as	ri in mer***ri***ly.
ṛī	as	ri in ma***ri***ne.
e	as	e in pr***e***y.
ai	as	ai in ***ai***sle.
o	as	o in st***o***ne.
au	as	ou in h***ou***se.
ś	as	s in ***s***ure.
ṣ	as	sh in ***sh***un, bu***sh***.
s	as	s in ***s***aint, ***s***un.

Introduction

In the summer of 1987, Swamiji began compiling what he considered to be the most important verses (*śloka*s) from the various scriptures (*śāstra*s) that he had studied throughout his life. Although these verses are primarily from Kashmir Shaivite sources, Swamiji also included verses from Vedāntic texts such as the *Yoga Vāsiṣtha* and the *Rāmāyaṇa*. Every Sunday, he would reveal the meaning of one or two of these verses to his devotees in Kashmir.

The following year, Swamiji traveled to Nepal with his nephew, Inder Krishen Raina, to meet with John and Denise Hughes and their two children with the express intent of sharing these important verses with them. He gave daily lectures, translating and explaining the essence of these verses. We are eternally grateful to John for his vigilance in recording Swamiji's revelation of these special verses.

During one of Swamiji's lectures, John asked him why he had compiled these different verses. Swamiji replied, "I compiled these *śloka*s with the intention of sharing them with you." When asked about the references for these verses, Swamiji said, "It is not for research. It is for your daily recitation. Maybe sometime you will experience these stages. Treat it as another independent book for your recitation. It will be helpful to you in *sādhana* (contemplative practice)."

As with other texts published by the Lakshmanjoo Academy, this book, *The Wisdom of Kashmir Shaivism*, is a carefully edited transcript along with footnotes for further clarification, the bulk of which are extracts from Swamiji's own explanations. The appendix includes a list of the *Wisdom Verses* without translations. Swamiji also made a separate audio recording of these verses in order to convey their correct pronunciation. Also included in the appendix are translations of the *Krama Stotra*, a treatise on the Twelve Kālīs, Abhinavagupta's *Anuttarāṣṭikā* (Eight Verses on the Supreme), the *Bhairava Stotra* (Hymn to Bhairava), the *Dehasthadevatācakra Stotra* (Hymn to the Gods and Goddesses Residing in One's Own Body), and *The Sixteen Amṛta*s (Nectars). We have provided links for downloadable audio and streaming video of the lectures which comprise this volume.

On behalf of the Lakshmanjoo Academy and the Universal Shaiva Fellowship, this precious gift from His Holiness is now available to all spiritual seekers.

God bless…
The Lakshmanjoo Academy Team

Acknowledgments

First of all, I would like to thank our associate editors: John Hughes, George Barselaar, and Denise Hughes. They took the raw unedited video and audio transcript and transformed it into a polished document ready for publication. Being closely attuned to Swamiji's vision, they were able to lightly edit the manuscript without tarnishing the flow of the narrative. Recognizing that these revelations were meant to aid the student in gaining a deeper understanding of the philosophy and practices of Kashmir Shaivism, comprehensive footnotes and an appendix have been added. Lastly, I would like to thank Michael Van Winkle, our audio engineer who enhanced the original audio, Aaron Kent for his video editing, Claudia Dose, our creative director who was responsible for the creation of the overall design of this book, George Barselaar for transcribing all of Swamiji's revelations, Nuno Ribeiro for typesetting and Shanna Hughes who coordinated this project.

Swami Lakshmanjoo

Swami Lakshmanjoo

Swami Lakshmanjoo was born in Srinagar, Kashmir, on May 9, 1907. He was the most recent and the greatest of the long line of saints and masters of the Kashmir Shaiva tradition. From a young age, Swami Lakshmanjoo spent his life studying and practicing the teachings of this unique and sacred tradition. Having a complete intellectual and spiritual understanding of the philosophy and practice of Kashmir Shaivism, he was a true master in every respect.

Endowed with a photographic memory, learning was always easy for Swamiji. In addition to possessing a complete knowledge of Kashmir Shaivism, he had a vast knowledge of the traditional religious and philosophical schools and texts of India. Swamiji would freely draw upon other texts to clarify, expand, and substantiate his lectures. He could recall an entire text by simply remembering the first few words of a verse.

In time, his reputation as a learned philosopher and spiritual adept spread. Spiritual leaders and scholars journeyed from all over the world to receive his blessings and to ask questions about various aspects of Kashmir Shaiva philosophy. He gained renown as a humble devotee of Lord Shiva and as an accomplished master (*siddha*) of the non-dual tradition of Kashmir Shaivism.

Throughout his life, Swamiji taught his disciples and devotees the ways of devotion and awareness. He shunned fame and all forms of recognition. He knew Kashmir Shaivism was the most precious jewel and that, by God's grace, those who desired supreme knowledge would be attracted to its teachings. He taught freely, never asking anything in return, except that his students, young and old, should do their utmost to assimilate the teachings of his cherished tradition. His earnest wish was for Kashmir Shaivism to be preserved and made available to all humankind.

On the 27th of September, 1991, Swami Lakshmanjoo left his physical body and attained *mahāsamādhi*, the great liberation.

Swami Lakshmanjoo

The Wisdom of Kashmir Shaivism

Compiled and Revealed by His Holiness, Swami Lakshmanjoo
Kathmandu, Nepal, July 1988

Wisdom Verses 1 (00:12)

SWAMIJI:

अस्तङ्गतवति प्राणे त्वपानेऽभ्युदयोन्मुखे ।
तावत्सा कुम्भकावस्था योगिभिरानुभूयते ॥ १ ॥

astaṅgatavati prāṇe tvapāne'bhyudayonmukhe /
tāvatsā kumbhakāvasthā yogibhirānubhūyate //1//

Is it alright if I say only once?

JOHN: Yes, anything you want, Sir.

SWAMIJI: Huh?

JOHN: Yes, Sir.

SWAMIJI: Have I to…? I will translate it also.

JOHN: Yes, please, yes.

SWAMIJI: *Astaṅgatavati prāṇe*, where is *prāṇa* (the outgoing breath), when the outgoing breath is finished, the movement of outgoing breath is finished, *tvapāne'bhyudayon-mukhe*, and the movement of the ingoing breath is to take place, has not taken place yet, but is to take place, at that point (*tāvat*, at that point), *sā kumbhakāvāsthā*, this automatic pause, *yogibhir ānubhūyate*, yogis have experienced it, that automatic pause. That automatic pause [between] these two breaths is really to be meditated upon. If you are not one-pointed on that automatic pause with each and every breath, nothing will happen. Yogis are bent upon finding out and searching and meditating upon that automatic pause. That automatic pause is just for one second, less than one second.[1]

---

1. "This junction is actually the fourth state, *turya*." *The Secret Supreme*. "That

He gives an example for this in another *śloka*:

Wisdom Verses 1 (02:18)

यथा निमीलने काले प्रपञ्चो नैव दृश्यते ।
तथौवोन्मीलने स्याच्चेदेतद्ध्यानस्य लक्षणम् ॥ २ ॥

yathā nimīlane kāle prapañco naiva dṛśyate /
tathaivonmīlane syāccedetatdhyānasya lakṣaṇam //2//

Yathā, just as, *nimīlane kāle*, when you close your eyes, when you close your eyes, at that moment, *prapañco naiva dṛśyate*, you cannot see anything what is outside in this world–when you close your eyes. *Tathaiva unmīlane syāt ced*, if that position takes place at the time when your eyes are open, although your eyes are open you don't see anything, *etat dhyānasya lakṣaṇam*, this is the actual test of *dhyāna* (meditation). Meditation must be like that. When you keep your eyes wide open and you don't see anything, you don't see anything with wide-opened eyes, that is the first test of your *dhyāna* (contemplation). That way, *dhyāna* must take place. You must meditate on that internal point, the junction, that pause, automatic pause, in such a way [that] it must go on in continuity of meditation. At that time, you won't see anything although your eyes are open. This is the meaning of the second verse.

---

junction is called *pramātraṁ śamātra*, there is subjective consciousness (*ahaṁ*) residing there." *Tantrāloka* 5.44 (LJA archive). Swamiji composed a poem with regard to this junction: "There is a point between sleep and waking where you must remain alert without shaking. Enter into the new world where hideous forms will pass. Endure. Do not be taken by the dross. Then the pulls and pushes about the throttle, all those you must tolerate. Close all ingress and egress. Yawnings there may be. Shed tears, crave, implore, and you will not prostrate. A thrill passes and that goes down to the bottom. It rises. May it bloom forth. That is Bliss. Blessed Being! Blessed Being! O greetings be to Thee!" Swami Lakshmanjoo, *Self-Realization in Kashmir Shaivism*, "Talks on Practice", 45-46.

Wisdom Verses 1 (04:41)

प्रकाशमाने परमार्थभानौ नश्यत्यविद्यातिमिरे समस्ते ।
तदा बुधाः निर्मलदृष्टयोऽपि किञ्चिन्न पश्यन्ति भवप्रपञ्चम्
॥ ३ ॥

prakāśamāne paramārthabhānau naśyatyavidyātimire samaste /
tadā budhā nirmaladṛṣtayo'pi kiñcinna paśyantī bhavaprapañcam //3//

This is the way how you should recite it, this *śloka*.

Prakāśamāne paramārthabhānau, paramārthabhānau, when the actual sun of God consciousness has risen, when the actual sun…*

Sun means, the sun. Which sun?

DENISE: Actual sun?

SWAMIJI: Actual sun, yes.

*…when the actual sun of God consciousness has risen, *naśyatyavidyātimire samaste*, at that time (*samaste*), all *avidyātimire*, all darkness of ignorance, *naśyati*, is vanished altogether. You can't find any darkness of ignorance there when that sun has risen, [when] the sun of God consciousness has risen. *Tadā*, at that moment, *budhā*, those who are elevated (yogis), *nirmala dṛṣtayo'pi*, although their eyes are wide open, *kiñcit na paśyantī bhavaprapañcam*, they don't find any existence of *saṁsāra*[2] before them. They find only God consciousness from all sides; in the front, in the backside, in the right side, in the left side, in the corners, they find only the glamour of God consciousness everywhere. So they don't find anything of those worldly things. Worldly things are gone for them for good.

2. The cycle of worldly existence.

Wisdom Verses 1 (07:22)

प्रनष्टवायुसञ्चारः पाषाण इव निश्चलः ।
परजीवैक्यधर्मज्ञो योगी योगविदुच्यते ॥४॥

pranaṣṭavāyusañcāraḥ pāṣāṇa iva niścalaḥ /
parajīvaikyadharmajñyo yogī yoga viducyate //4//

This is the position of a yogi when he is sunk in God consciousness, what happens to him. He explains this.

Praṇaṣṭa vāyu sañcāraḥ, the in-going breathing and the out-coming breath, the out-coming breath and the in-going breath has absolutely stopped, there is no breathing inside and outside, when the breath has already stopped (*praṇaṣṭa vāyu sañcāraḥ*, *vāyu sañcāraḥ* means the movement of breath inside and outside, as you breathe, as we breath inside and outside), when this movement of breath is totally finished, *pāṣāṇa iva niścalaḥ*, he becomes just like a rock, the yogi becomes, at that time, just like a rock, *niścalaḥ*, without any movement altogether. He cannot move his body at all, he is just like a rock. But, at the same time, he is not just like a rock just like a dead body. *Para jīvaikya dharmajñyo*, he finds the unification of the individual in universal consciousness; at that time, he experiences the union of individual consciousness with universal consciousness. That kind of yogi is [said] to be a perfect yogi.

Have you understood?

Wisdom Verses 1 (9:46)

ब्रह्मविष्णुमहेशादिदेवता भूतजातयः ।
नाशमेवानुधावन्ति तस्माच्छ्रेयः समभ्यसेत् ॥५॥

brahma viṣṇumaheśādi devatā bhūtajātayaḥ /
nāśamevānudhāvanti tasmācchreyaḥ samabhyaset //5//

Brahma, Viṣṇu, Maheśa *ādi*, and Rudra, all *devatā bhūtajātaya*, all those gods, heavenly gods, and *bhūtajātaya*, all individuals, *nāśam eva anudhāvanti*, get their end in there own time–they die. Brahma also dies, Viṣṇu also dies when the time comes, and Rudra also dies when the time comes, and all individuals die when their time comes. *Nāśam eva anudhāvanti*, they are destroyed, they are finished. *Tasmāt*, so, *śreyaḥ samabhyaset*, you must find out and research for *śreya*, the perfect achievement of God consciousness where the cycle of repeated births and deaths (*saṁsāra*) is put to its end for good. This is another *śloka*.

Now, in the next *śloka* he explains: the individual has nothing in his power. As long as individuality is concerned, for an individual being, he is powerless himself (laughs). He cannot do according to his choice. If [God] wishes, it can be washed off by God consciousness if He so likes. This is what he says:

Wisdom Verses 1 (11:59)

अज्ञो जन्तुरनीशोऽयमात्मनः सुखदुःखयोः ।
ईश्वरप्रेरितो गच्छेत् श्वभ्रं वा स्वर्गमेव वा ॥६॥

ajño janturanīśo'yamātmanaḥ sukhaduḥkhayoḥ /
īśvaraprerito gacchet śvabhraṁ vā svargameva vā //6//

Ajña jantur, *jantur* (this individual) is *ajña* (ignorant). *Anīśo'yam*, he has no power. For what? *Ātmanaḥ sukha duḥkhayoḥ*, to [control] his pains and pleasures of this world. If pleasures come, he cannot keep them in a stable condition, they will go, from his hands they will be lost. They will remain for sometime, [the duration of] which he doesn't know. He thinks that it will remain always, but it does not remain. So he is *asvatantra* (dependent); *anīśo* means, he has no power to keep it like this. Or *duḥkha* (pain), pain also he cannot…

JOHN: Get rid of?

SWAMIJI:…get rid of according to his choice. As long as pain is concerned, pain will remain there. And it will go according to the choice of Lord Śiva, not according to the choice of the individual.

So *īśvara prerito gacchet*, wherever Īśvara (God) kicks him, he is thrown there, *śvabhraṁ vā* (in hell), *svargameva* (or heaven)–*śvabhraṁ vā svargameva vā* (*śvarga* means, heaven).

JOHN: "*Śva bharaṁ*" or "*bhram*"? Is this "*śvabharam*"?

SWAMIJI: *Śvabhraṁ, śvabhraṁ.*

JOHN: Is it a misspelling here? Is it wrong?

SWAMIJI: No, it is all right like this. You have to listen from that tape recorder [for] the pronunciation as I have pronounced. Don't go in the depth of these…

VIRESH: Words.

SWAMIJI:…words.

Wisdom Verses 1 (14:40)

यावन्नैव प्रविशति चरन्मरुतो मध्यमार्गे ।
यावद्बिन्दुर्न भवति दृढं प्राणवातप्रबन्धात् ॥७॥
यावन्नैव सहजसदृशं जायते चैव तत्त्वं ।
तावत्सर्वं तदिदमखिलं दम्भमिथ्याप्रलापम् ॥८॥

yāvannaiva praviśati caran maruto madhyamārge /
yāvat bindur na bhavati dṛḍhaṁ prāṇavāta prabandhāt //7//
yāvannaiva sahajasadṛśaṁ jāyate caiva tattvaṁ /
tāvat sarvaṁ tadidamakhilaṁ dambhamithyāpralāpam //8//

Yāvat, as long as, *naiva praviśati caran maruto madhya-mārge*, *caran maruto*, *caran*, the movement of breath, as long as the movement of breath, in-going and out-coming both, these breaths, as long as these two breaths do not enter in the central vein automatically by the force of one-pointedness, as long as it does not take place,…

What?

JOHN: Enter in the central vein by one-pointedness automatically?

SWAMIJI:...[as long as] it does not enter in that,[3] *yāvat bindur na bhavati dṛḍhaṁ prāṇavāta prabandhāt, prāṇavāta prabandhāt*, by the continuity of inhaling and exhaling, inhaling and exhaling with the force of meditation, when by the continuity of inhaling and exhaling with awareness, *bindur na bhavati dṛḍhaṁ, bindur*, that one-pointedness, that point between two eyebrows does not take place firmly at one point, as long as it does not take place, as long as that breath does not enter in that central vein, as long as this point between the eyebrows does not get perfectly established in one point, *yāvat naiva*, and at the same time, as long as *naiva sahajasadṛśaṁ jāyate caiva tattvaṁ*, the reality of God consciousness, the glamour of God consciousness, as long as that is not experienced after this happening, in fullness of ecstasy, *tāvat*, till then, *tat sarvaṁ tadidamakhilaṁ*, whatever you do in this world (you deliver lectures, you deliver gatherings, and festivals of seminars, and propagation of Śaivism), all this *tamāśā* (drama), *dambha mithyāpralāpam*, it is just [hypocrisy] and with no fruit [coming] out of it. No fruit comes as long as this does not happen, this does not take place.

Karan Singh once managed a seminar in Gupta Ganga–you were in the United States [at that time]–and I was supposed to participate in that seminar of Śaivism at Gupta Ganga. It was just one day after the *jag*, I don't know when, perhaps last year. I told them this *śloka*, I recited this *śloka* to all those scholars of Śaivism. Some were of the *Pratyabhijñā Darśan* (the school of Recognition) and some were of...they were all fools according to my understanding. I told them, I abused them. And this...

DENISE: Karan Singh?

SWAMIJI: No, Karan Singh was not there. Baljināth Pandit kept quiet in one corner. I was furious with all! I said, "Nothing will happen to you. You are only talking nonsense. What will you do? This is not

3. Also known as *madhyanāḍī* or *suṣumnā*, "in that central vein is situated that goddess Kālakarṣiṇī, Kālasaṁkarṣiṇī. Kālasaṁkarṣiṇī is that goddess who digest time, dissolves time, absorbs time. When that Kālasaṁkārṣiṇī takes the formation of *urdhva recaka bhāva*, it flows up from the central vein from the rectum to *sahasrāra*. When, by *urdhva recaka*, it rises up, *utthitā kṣaṇāt kālaṁ saṁgrasate*, then She destroys the cycle of this threefold time (there is no in-going breath, out-coming breath, or center-junction). *Tantrāloka* 15.336-337 (LJA archive).

the real point of Śaivism that you are doing." And they all kept quiet. Perhaps [Inderji] was also there.

INDERJI: I was there. It was a question and answer session for about two hours.

SWAMIJI: Questions and answers, *bas*.

JOHN: Two hours of questions and answers? Who was asking questions?

SWAMIJI: Those scholars.

INDERJI: It was conducted by the university of Jammu and Kashmir.

JOHN: So they were asking you questions?

SWAMIJI: Yes. I would answer them and beat them thoroughly for those questions. Those questions were odd.

JOHN: Odd questions (laughs).

SWAMIJI: Yes, baseless questions.

INDERJI: The crux was whether the experience is important or the reading is important. Am I right, Sir?

SWAMIJI: Yes. I told them, "Unless you have got experience, you will gain nothing, it is useless, a waste of time of holding seminars and…it is all *bakwas* (nonsense)."

INDERJI: Then many came to the Ashram that day, the following day, on Sunday.

SWAMIJI:

Wisdom Verses 1 (22:07)

आश्यानं चिद्रसस्यौघं साकारत्वमुपागतम् ।
जगद्रूपतया वन्दे प्रत्यक्षं भैरवं वपुः ॥९॥

āśyānaṁ cidrasasyaughaṁ sākāratvamupāgatam /
jagadrūpatayā vande pratyakṣaṁ bhairavaṁ vapuḥ //9//

Cidrasasyaugham aśyānam, *cidrasa*, the coagulation of *cit rasa*[4] is called the universe, is the universe, it is not anything else than God consciousness. It is just God consciousness but coagulated consciousness. Coagulated means that it is just like it becomes hard to experience.

JOHN: Hard to experience?

SWAMIJI: It has become hard by coagulation[5], but actually this is also God consciousness. The manifestation of this whole universe is God consciousness. *Sākāratvam upāgatam*, and it has taken its [differentiated] formation–this is Viresh, this is Denise, this is Shanna, this is Inderji, this is Lakṣmanjoo, this is John. It has taken this formation. What?

DENISE: This universe.

SWAMIJI: No.

JOHN: This coagulation of *cid rasa*.

SWAMIJI: God consciousness. God consciousness has been coagulated in these varieties of forms and shapes and time. *Sākāratvam upāgatam*, it has taken its shape, *jagad rūpatayā*, in the formation of the universe. So the universe is, in another way, the universe is no other than God consciousness. It is God consciousness–this universe. It is the commentary of God consciousness. It is the manifestation of God consciousness in its coagulated form. *Jagadrūpatayā vande*, so, we must embrace it, we must hug it, we must not throw it away. It is not a dream, this world is not a dream. This is just God consciousness.

JOHN: Or illusion, it's not illusion.

SWAMIJI: It is not illusion. *Jagadrūpatayā vande*, I bow to this universe, which is *pratyakṣam bhairavam vapuḥ*, this Bhairava has come with formation. This Bhairava can be photographed, and that Bhairava cannot be photographed, which is…

JOHN: Transcendental.

DENISE: Transcendental.

SWAMIJI: That is transcendental. So this [universe] is also Bhairava. You must not be afraid of this God consciousness which is coagulated in the formation of *saṁsāra*. So you should not get afraid

---

4. The fluid, nectar or taste (*rasa*) of God consciousness (*cit*), the *ānanda* of God consciousness.

5. *Aśyāna* literally means, shrunk or dried up.

from *saṁsāra*. There is no question, there is no room for fearing this universe. Because the universe, as long as it is concerned, it is the actual formation of God consciousness in coagulated form. That is the only difference. This is the *śloka* which…

āśyānaṁ cidrasasyaughaṁ sākāratvamupāgatam /
jagadrūpatayā vande pratyakṣaṁ bhairavaṁ vapuḥ //9//
(repeated)

Wisdom Verses 1 (26:08)

उज्झित्वात्मसमाधानं ये ध्यायन्त्यन्यदेवताः ।
भिक्ष्यन्ते भूरिवित्तास्ते भिक्षित्वापि बुभुक्षिताः ॥ १० ॥

ujjhitvātma samādhānaṁ ye dhyāyantyanyadevatāḥ /
bhikṣyante bhūrivittāste bhikṣitvāpi bubhukṣitāḥ //10//

Ujjhitvātma samādhānaṁ, ātma samādhānaṁ ujjitva, after putting aside concentration upon your own nature, if one puts aside the concentration upon his own nature, those people (*ye*, those people), *dhyāyanti anya devatāḥ*, go and contemplate other gods (other gods, say except your own Self, real Self, Self of God consciousness), those people who leave that God consciousness of Self aside and are bent upon meditating upon other gods (for instance, Brahma, Viṣṇu, even individual gods, Rajiv Gandhi, Sonya Gandhi, they take refuge in those gods), those people who leave aside the *ātma samādhāna*, the reality of one's own God consciousness, who leaves that aside, who does not think of that, and they go to search other gods, those persons who take refuge in these gods and leave aside the God who is within them, *bhikṣyante*, they are just begging, they are just begging. *Bhūrivittāste*, they are well-off, their bank balance is filled internally. Who?

JOHN: Those people who neglect their own Self and seek refuge in other gods.

SWAMIJI: Yes. *Bhūrivittāste*, they have got *bhūrivittāste*, they have got sufficient money within their own self. "Money" does not mean these coins. Money means…

DENISE: Spiritual treasure?

SWAMIJI: Yes. *Bhikṣitvāpi*, although they beg from other gods, *bhikṣitvāpi bubhukṣitā*, they are always begging, their begging does not take its end. So you should not beg. You should see your own bank balance, what it is. [It is] so much that you will never lose it.

Avasthā bheda prakriyā, this is *avasthā bheda prakriyā*, these states, the five states [of] wakefulness, dreaming state, dreamless state, and *turya* and *turyātīta*, these five states are:

Wisdom Verses 1 (30:07)

Avasthā Bheda Prakriyā
The Paths of the States (of Consciousness)

जाग्रत्स्वप्नसुषुप्तान्यत्तदतीतानि यान्यपि ।
तान्यप्यमुष्यनाथस्य स्वातन्त्र्यलहरीभरः ॥ ११ ॥

jāgrat svapnasuṣuptānyattadatītāni yānyapi /
tānyapyamuṣyanāthasya svātantryalaharībharaḥ //11//

Jāgrat (waking state), *svapna* (dreaming state), *suṣupta* (dreamless state), *anya* (*turya* state; *anya* means, another one, the fourth one), *tadatītāni* (above the fourth–*turyātīta*), *yānyapi*, all these five states which are existing in this universe, *tāni*, all those states are *amuṣyanāthasya svātantryala harī bharaḥ*, the tides and waves, continuous tides and waves of His *svātantrya śakti*.[6] These are tides, these are nothing other than the tides of God consciousness–these five states. Wakefulness is one big tide, the dreaming state is a tide of God consciousness, the dreamless state is a tide of God consciousness–you know "tide"?–and *turya* is a tide of God consciousness, and *turyātīta* is a tide of God consciousness in its fullness. That is explained in:

---

6. Energy of supreme independence.

jāgrat svapnasuṣuptānyattadatītāni yānyapi /
tānyapyamuṣyanāthasya svātantryalaharībharaḥ //11//
(repeated)

Now *pramātṛ bheda prakriyā*. Now he refers to the seven *pramātṛ*s (perceivers): *sakala*, *pralayākala*, *vijñānākala*, *mantra*, *mantreśvara*, *mantra maheśvara*,...

JOHN:...and Śakti and Śiva.

SWAMIJI: Yes.

Wisdom Verses 1 (32:19)

Pramātṛ Bheda Prakriyā
The Paths of Subjectivity

महामन्त्रेशमन्त्रेशमन्त्राः शिवपुरोगमाः ।
अकलौ सकलश्चेति शिवस्यैव विभूतयः ॥१२॥

mahāmantreśamantreśa mantrāḥ śivapurogamāḥ /
akalau sakalaśceti śivasyaiva vibhūtayaḥ //12//

Mahā mantreśa; *mahā mantreśa* means, *mantra maheśvara*, the state of Sadāśiva. *Mantreśa* [is] the state of Īśvara. *Mantra* [is] the state of Śuddhavidyā. *Śivapurogamaḥ*, and Śiva. How many are they? *Mahā mantreśa*, *mantra maheśvara* is one. *Mantreśvara* (Īśvara) is second. *Mantra*...

JOHN: Śuddhavidyā.

SWAMIJI:...is third. Śiva is fourth. *Akalau* means, *vijñānākala* and *pralayākala* (the fifth and sixth). *Sakalaśca*, and *sakala* (*sakala* is the seventh). And these seven states of *pramātṛ bhava*, *śivasyaiva vibhūtaya*, are just the glory of Lord Śiva, nothing else. So, if you have to see the glory of Lord Śiva, see the glory of Lord Śiva in wakefulness, see the glory of Lord Śiva in these all seven *pramātṛ bhava*s, in *sakala*. We are in *sakala*. At the time of deep sleep, we are in *pralayākala*. At the time of entrance to God consciousness, we are in *vijñānākala*. At the time of experiencing God consciousness, we are in Śuddhavidyā. At the time of fullness of God consciousness, we are in Īśvara. At the time of complete fullness of God consciousness, we are in Sadāśiva. At the time of glamour of Śiva, we are in Śiva *bhava*. And all these are no less than each other, they are just *vibhūti*, they are glamour, seven ways of the glamour of God consciousness. So don't worry about experiencing Śiva. If you are experiencing *sakala*, that is also fine, no worry.

mahāmantreśamantreśa mantrāḥ śivapurogamāḥ /
akalau sakalaśceti śivasyaiva vibhūtayaḥ //12//
(repeated)

Now *kṛtya bheda prakaraṇam*. *Kṛtya bheda prakaraṇam* is just the five acts of Lord Śiva: creation, protection, destruction,...

JOHN: Concealing and revealing.

SWAMIJI:...concealing and revealing.

Wisdom Verses 1 (35:38)

Kṛtya Bheda Prakriyā
The Paths of Action

सृष्टिस्थितितिरोधान संहारानुग्रहादि च ।
तुर्यमित्यपि देवस्य बहुशक्तित्वजृम्भितम् ॥ १३ ॥

sṛṣtisthititirodhāna saṁhārānugrahādi ca /
turyamityapi devasya bahuśaktitvajṛmbhitam //13//

Sṛṣṭi means creation, *sthiti* means protection, *tirodhāna* is [concealing], *saṁhāra* is destruction, *anugrahādi ca*, and *anugraha* [is revealing]. These five acts of Lord Śiva, *turyamityapi*, and actually these five acts are residing in *turya*, in God consciousness. *Sṛṣṭi* (creation) is in God consciousness, protection is in God consciousness, and *saṁhāra* (destruction) is in God consciousness, concealing is in

God consciousness, and revealing is in God consciousness. For this purpose he has put the sixth one. The sixth one is *turya*. *Turya* is the basis of all these five acts of Lord Śiva. These five acts are *devasya*, of the Lord, *bahu śakti tvajṛmbhitam*, just the glamour of His energies.

Wisdom Verses 1 (37:23)

Dvādaśakālīnāṁ Prādubhāvasthitiḥ
The Rise of the Twelve Kālīs

तस्य शक्तय एवैतास्तिस्रो भान्ति परादिकाः ।
सृष्टौ स्थितौ लये तुर्ये तेनैताः द्वादशोदिताः ॥ १४ ॥

tasya śaktaya evaitāstisro bhānti parādikāḥ /
srṣṭau sthitau laye turye tenaitāḥ dvādaśoditāḥ //14//

I'll recite this twice so you can repeatedly…

JOHN: Understand it.

SWAMIJI:…again learn, understand. Now this is here in this *śloka*, is the reference given that these twelve Kālīs, the twelve Kālīs are produced by Lord Śiva. You know the Kālīs? The twelve Kālīs.

Etāstisro śaktaya tasya, *tasya*, these three energies of Lord Śiva, *parā śakti*, *parāparā śakti*, and *aparā śakti* (*parā śakti* is supreme *śakti*, and *parāparā śakti* is medium *śakti*, and *aparā śakti* is inferior *śakti*; He has got three energies, these *śakti*s: *parā*, *parāparā*, and *aparā*), and these three *śakti*s are manifested by His *svātantrya śakti*, *srṣṭau* (in the act of creation), *sthitau* (in the act of protection), *laye* (in the act of destruction), and in the act of God consciousness (*turye*).

JOHN: Swamiji, could you say something for Viresh and Shanna about what this *svātantrya śakti* is?

SWAMIJI: *Svātantrya śakti* is His free will. Whatever He wishes, that is *svātantrya śakti*. *Svātantrya śakti* is the germ of all His five energies. He has got five energies: *cit śakti* (energy of consciousness), *ānanda śakti* (energy of bliss)–they are two–energy of will (third), energy of knowledge (fourth), and energy of action (fifth). All these five energies of God consciousness are produced by His *svātantrya śakti*, of [His] freedom, it is [His] free power. That is called *svātantrya śakti. Svātantrya śakti* produces these five energies of Lord Śiva. And *cit śakti* is actually based on His nature. *Ānanda śakti* is based on His *śakti*, on His Pārvatī. *Icchā śakti* is based on Sadāśiva. And *jñāna śakti* (the energy of knowledge) is based on Īśvara. And the energy of *kriyā* is based of Śuddhavidyā. All these five pure states of Lord Śiva are one with Lord Śiva. *Cit śakti* indicates Lord Śiva's actual position. *Ānanda śakti* indicates Lord Śiva's position of Śakti. And *icchā śakti* indicates Lord Śiva's position of Sadāśiva. And *jñāna śakti* indicates His position in Īśvara, the Īśvara state. And Śuddhavidyā is the fifth position. All these five positions are filled with God consciousness. Below that is the scale of *māyā* (illusion), that will go from *māyā* to earth. For that we have nothing to do here.

And these three energies of Lord Śiva (*parā*, *parāparā*, and *āpara*) are manifested in the action of creation, in the action of protection, in the action of destruction, and in the action of God consciousness. Four. Four into three?

SHANNA: Twelve.

SWAMIJI: Huh?

DENISE: Three times four?

SWAMIJI: Four into three.

JOHN: Twelve.

SWAMIJI: *Tena*, this way, *etāḥ*, these energies, become *dvādaśo*, twelve energies. And those are supposed to be the twelve Kālīs of Lord Śiva which have been produced by His three energies (*parā*, *parāparā*, and *aparā*) by the unification of creation, protection, destruction, and *turya* (God consciousness). So they become twelve. These twelve energies are explained in *śāktopāya* (chapter 4) of the *Tantrāloka*. You'll find those there.

Wisdom Verses 1 (43:35)

ADHVA BHEDA PRAKRIYĀ
THE PATHS OF THE ORBITS

बहुशक्तित्वमस्योक्तं शिवस्य यदतो महान् ।
कलातत्त्वपुरार्णाणुपदादिर्भेदविस्तरः ॥ १५॥

bahuśaktitvamasyoktaṁ śivasya yadato mahān /
kalātattvapurārṇāṇupadādirbhedavistaraḥ //15//

Bahu śaktitvamasyoktaṁ, Lord Śiva is supposed to be the possessor of numberless energies! *Bahu śaktitvamasyoktaṁ*, He has numberless, He has not only these energies which have been explained here. He has numberless energies. In this way, He is supposed to be *mahān*, greater than the greatest in all respects. He is greater than the greatest. Anything greatest you find in this world, He is greater than that, a little bit greater than that. So he is greater. Comparative degrees found to be the…subsiding the highest quality of the superlative degree, it subsides the superlative degree in the end. Superlative degree is?

JOHN: The most.

SWAMIJI: Most.

JOHN: He is more than the most.

SWAMIJI: He is more than most (laughs). This way, in…unfortunately you couldn't go on with the explanation of the *Parātrīṁśikā Vivaraṇa* the last day, when we had that book to explain.

JOHN: It is almost finished, isn't it?

SWAMIJI: No. It is partly finished. So He is supposed to be greater than the greatest. Who?

DENISE: Lord Śiva.

SWAMIJI: Lord Śiva. *Kalā tattva purārṇāṇu padādiḥ bheda vistaraḥ. Kalā* [means], *kalādhva* (five circles). *Tattva* means, *tattvādhva* (36 *tattvas*). *Pura* means, *bhuvanādhva* (118 worlds). *Aṇu* means, *mantrādhva* (world of words). *Padādi* means, *padādhva* (world of sentences). And *ādi* means, etcetera, that is, *varṇādhva* (world of letters).

So this world of five *kalās* [contain the] thirty-six elements. The five *kalās* are supposed to be *nivṛtti kalā*, *pratiṣṭhā kalā*, *vidyā kalā*, *śāntā kalā*, *śāntātītā kalā*–these five circles. In which five circles you find the thirty-six elements, that is the *tattvas*, that is called *tattvādhva*. *Kalādhva* is those five circles (*nivṛtti kalā*, *pratiṣṭhā kalā*, *vidyā kalā*, *śāntā kalā*, and *śāntātītā kalā*). You have been explained, I have explained this to you.

JOHN: Yes, Sir.

SWAMIJI: By "*kalā*" you should put those "five circles". In "*tattva*, *tattvādhva*" you will put "thirty-six elements." *Pura*, or "*bhuvanādhva*" you should put "one hundred and eighteen worlds." One hundred and eighteen worlds, thirty-six elements, and five circles. That is *kalā*, *tattva*, *pura*, then *arṇa*; *arṇa* means, letter, word, and sentences. This is letters, words and sentences, It is called *vācakādhva*. *Vācakādhva* [means], it speaks, it explains what is what. For instance, this [tape recorder] is what you feel here. This is *vācyādhva*. This will come either in *kalā*, or in the thirty-six elements (*tattvādhva*), or in one hundred and eighteen worlds–this [tape recorder]. And its speaker is "tape recorder," this word. This is its speaker. It will come in *vācakādhva*, the speaker's world. The speaker's world is something else. For instance, this is this [body of Shanna]. Of this, the speaker is, "body of Shanna"–this is speaker. The speaker of [Viresh's] body is, "this body is of Viresh." [The speaker of Denise's body is], "this body is of Denise." This is the speaker. This will come in *vācakādhva*. And this will come either in the five *kalās*, or the thirty-six elements, or one hundred and eighteen worlds. The speaked, what is spoken, what is spoken is that first three–*vācya*. And *vācaka* is the speaker.[7]

---

7. "This course of the threefold *adhvans* is called *vācyādhva*. The word *vācya* means, that which is observed, spoken, told. So *vācyādhva* is the path of that which is observed, seen, realized. It is called *vācyādhva* because it is seen, it is observed, it is created, it is felt. It is the objective cycle of this creation. Now, we must turn to its observer, the creator of this *adhvan*. The creator of the threefold path of the universe is called *vācakādhva*. The meaning of the word *vācaka* is "that which observes, sees, and creates." And so that path which observes, sees, and creates is called *vācakādhva*. It is the subjective cycle of this creation. And, like *vācyādhva*, *vācakādhva* is also composed of three paths: gross (*sthūla*), subtle (*sūkṣma*),

This *bheda vistara*, this differentiated position of this world in the speaker section and that which is spoken by the speakers, this is just the glory of Lord Śiva. The five circles (*kalās*), the thirty-six elements (*tattvas*), and one hundred and eighteen worlds (*bhuvanas*), and along with letters, words, and sentences (these are speakers, this is the world of the speaker), this is just the glory of Lord Śiva.

JOHN: Things and their names.

SWAMIJI: Huh?

JOHN: The things themselves and the names we give those things.

SWAMIJI: "Things" you should not say. [Say] whatever it is. This [typed-paper]. What is its speaker? "Typed paper." "Typed paper" is its speaker. Speaker of what?

VIRESH: Typed-paper.

SWAMIJI: This [typed-paper]. Whenever you show this to a dog, he will see this.

JOHN: He won't say, "it's typed-paper."

SWAMIJI: He won't see its speaker. We have adjusted the speaker for this.

JOHN: The name.

SWAMIJI: The name, yes. This way, this whole world goes on.

JOHN: So things have real names or…?

SWAMIJI: No, they are adjusted, they are adjusted for our…

JOHN: Convenience or use.

SWAMIJI: For our use. Otherwise, those speakers also are in their own way untouched by the speaker. "Speaker," "speaker," this is only just a word. "Speaker" will [be understood by] a dog also–"speaker," this word, this sound–but the meaning is in *māyā*, in illusion. This will go in *vācakādhva*–the speaker, if it is a real speaker. Otherwise, this speaker itself, it is God consciousness, it has no meaning.

JOHN: So that's *nirvikalpa*.

SWAMIJI: That is *nirvikalpa* (thought-less).

---

and subtlest (*para*). Gross (*sthūla*) *vācakādhva* is called *padādhva* and consists of sentences (sentences are said to be gross). Subtle (*sūkṣma*) *vācakādhva* is called *mantrādhva* and consists of words because words are known to be more subtle than sentences. Subtler than *mantrādhva*, the world of words, is the path of letters called *varṇādhva*." *The Secret Supreme*, p. 12.

JOHN: And the other state is *savikalpa*, with some…
SWAMIJI: That is *savikalpa* (thought-full), yes. That is what he says here. This is the cream of Śaivism. Now, in another two *śloka*s is defined [how] in each and every way He is bent upon elevating people–in each and every way. If He punishes somebody in this world, it is to elevate him, it is for elevating him. He does good to everybody, in each and every being, who is created by Him. He wants to elevate him. He can elevate him in a good sense or He can elevate him by punishing [him] if he is unyielding for being elevated. If he is mostly given to worldly pleasures too much so [that] he is unyielding to get elevated, for him He gives some punishment so that [he will be elevated]. That punishment is also, in the long-run, for elevating him.

Wisdom Verses 1 (53:47) end
Wisdom Verses 2 (00:10) start

Śaktipātasya Vaicitryam
The Variations of Grace

कदाचिद्भक्तियोगेन कर्मणा विद्ययापि वा ।
ज्ञानधर्मोपदेशेन मन्त्रैर्वा दीक्षयापि वा ॥ १६ ॥
एवमाद्यैरनेकैश्च प्रकारैः परमेश्वरः ।
संसारिणोऽनुगृह्णाति विश्वस्य जगतः पतिः ॥ १७ ॥
(युगलकं)

kadācidbhaktiyogena karmaṇā vidyayāpi vā /
jñānadharmopadeśena mantrairvā dīkṣayāpi vā //16//
evamādyairanekaiśca prakāraiḥ parameśvaraḥ /
saṁsāriṇo'nugṛhṇāti viśvasya jagataḥ patiḥ //17//

Kadācit, sometime, *bhakti yogena*, by putting *bhakti*, intensity of devotion towards Himself, He elevates somebody–by putting in his mind the intensity of devotion towards the Lord. That is Bhakti Yoga. *Kadācit*, sometime by producing *bhakti* in him–sometime. And sometime *karmaṇā*, sometime with some good actions He elevates people, making him do good actions for the welfare of the world. He begins to do good actions for the welfare of the world. By that way He elevates him. The one who is not worthy of [practicing] yoga, for him He does elevate him this way. Which way? To make him do…

JOHN: Good actions.

SWAMIJI:…good actions so that he will rise. *Kadācit bhakti yogena, karmaṇa, vidyayāpi vā*, sometimes He elevates people by producing knowledge in him, the knowledge of what is right and what is wrong. By producing that knowledge in his mind, He elevates him. *Jñāna dharma upadeśena*, sometimes He elevates an individual being by initiating him in what is knowledge and what is duty, what is your duty in this world, what for you have been created, what for you have been situated in this world, what for you have come to live, by producing the background of this, what for you have to live in this world. You have not to live in this world to grow and to go to school, to get married, to go to the cinema, to go for dancing, and get old and die in the end. For that you have not been sent here. You have been sent here for developing an intense devotion towards the Lord at the same time, side-by-side. *Mantrairvā*, or He elevates people by initiating him with some mantra through some master. You must not think that when a master elevates you [that] actually the master elevates you. It is not the master, it is the elevating power [that] has been produced by Lord Śiva through the master to you. So you are elevated by Lord Śiva. Or *dīkṣayāpi vā*, just by initiating, by being initiated, He elevates. *Evamādyair anekaiśca prakāraiḥ*, this way, with many ways, Lord Śiva elevates *saṁsāriṇaḥ*, [those] who are worldly people, Lord Śiva elevates them. Each and everybody, He elevates them. If they are totally neglecting the position of Lord Śiva, neglecting the reality of this world, those also are elevated by Him by some punishment for the time-being so they will realize what they are doing [and understand], "We are not doing good actions." So He just elevates everybody. You must not think…without distinction, without distinction He elevates everybody. Because *viśvasya jagataḥ patiḥ*, He is the husband of the whole universe. He has to take care of what He has created. He has to see and watch that everything is going on nicely.

How beautiful *śloka*s are they? Now he says in another *śloka*: the reality of His nature has no succession.

Wisdom Verses 2 (06:46)

क्रमाभावान्न युगपत्तदभावात्क्रमोऽपि न ।
क्रमाक्रमकथातीतं संवित्तत्त्वं सुनिर्मलम् ॥ १८ ॥

kramābhāvānna yugapattadabhāvātkramo'pi na /
kramākramakathātītaṁ saṁvittattvaṁ sunirmalam //18//

Kramābhāvāt na yugapat, kramābhāvāt, there is no succession, when there is no succession [and when] simultaneous happening is not there–there is not succession, there is not non-succession (non-succession is simultaneously)–*tat abhāvāt kramo'pi na*, so when they are both absent (*kramo'pi na*, succession also fails there), *kramākrama kathātītaṁ*, so the purity of God consciousness is above this cycle of succession and the cycle of non-succession. Sometimes He is realized in a successive way (bit-by-bit), sometimes He is realized simultaneously. For instance, there is one blind person. A big elephant is put before him. He touches his tail. He does not know the remaining portion of the body of the elephant. He thinks that the elephant is just like a rope. Another blind person touches his legs. He thinks it is just like a log. This is the successive way. The simultaneous way is for those who are not blind. They see what is what, [that] the elephant is like this. They see the full shape of the elephant. That is beyond succession. That [previous way] is succession. That, too, is correct. You cannot deny that [the tail] is not [un]like a rope. It is just like a rope partly, it is just like a log partly, it is just like a mountain partly. When he touches its body, he thinks that it is a mountain, just like a mountain, like that. In the successive way also, it is correct; in non-succession (simultaneously), who are really realizing in the correct way, they also are correct. [Those] who are realizing partly, they are also correct. But one must think that *saṁvit tattva*, the essence of God consciousness, is very pure, very pure, it can be anything.

Wisdom Verses 2 (10:24)

अदीक्षितानां पुरतो नोच्चरेत् शिवसंहिताम् ।
तमाराध्य ततस्तुष्टाद्दीक्षामासाध्य शांकरीम् ॥ १९ ॥
येन केनाप्युपायेन गुरुमाराध्य भक्तितः ।
तद्दीक्षाक्रमयोगेन शास्त्रार्थं वेत्त्यसौ ततः ॥ २० ॥
अभिषेकं समासाध्य यो भवेत् स तु कल्पितः ।
सन्नप्यशेषापाशौघविनिवर्तनकोविदः ॥ २१ ॥
(तिलकं)

adīkṣitānāṁ purato noccaret śivasaṁhitām /
tamārādhya tatastuṣṭāddīkṣāmāsādhya śāṁkarīṁ //19//
yena kenāpyupāyena gurumārādhya bhaktitaḥ /
taddīkṣākramayogena śāstrārthaṁ vettyasau tataḥ //20//
abhiṣekaṁ samāsādhya yo bhavet sa tu kalpitaḥ /
sannapyaśeṣāpāśaughavinivartanakovidaḥ //21//

Bas, up to that, it is only one sentence.

Adīkṣitānāṁ purato noccaret śivasaṁhitām, *adīkṣitānāṁ purato*, those who are not initiated by masters (Śaivite masters), before them you should not utter the secret of Śaivism–before those rascals who are not initiated properly, who are initiated and have gone astray afterwards.

I had to give them a hint that you have been initiated by [me]–the people in Srinagar–I had to give them a hint that you have been initiated by me, and afterwards you have gone astray. So, before such people, you should not reveal the secret of Śaivism.

For possessing this secret of Śaivism, *tamārādhya*, you have to devote all your life before your master–*tamārādhya*. *Tatas tuṣṭāt*, then, when he will be pleased with you, *dīkṣāmāsādhya śāṁkarīṁ*, then he will properly initiate you. But for that initiation, you are not supposed to throw, place your money before him, you are not supposed to give a luxurious car to that master. *Yena kenāpyupāyena*–for that he says another *śloka–yena kenāpyupāyena gurumārādhya bhaktitaḥ*, whatever means you have to take to satisfy your master, you have to ask your master, "What kind of service do you need, Sir, from me?"–*yena kenāpyupāyena*, any service which is liked by the master. [That service] which is hated by the master, by that you'll just fall in the pit of ignorance. You have not to do with your own free will, you have not to serve your master with your own free will. You have to depend upon the choice of the master, which service he needs from you. For this, Abhinavagupta has explained: *kaścit hi dhanena*, some masters like money, they want money from their disciples, they are satisfied with that money–*kaścit hi dhanena. Kaścit hi sevayā*, some masters like your energy of life, you have to devote just service, you have to serve him with all your mind and body. Some masters like that service, they don't like money.

This way I told [my devotees]: "You get heaps of these offerings for me on every Sunday, [but] I don't like it. This way you will just be ruined. Don't get these things. I want your life to be wasted in my service. That is what I like. I don't want money, I don't want you to show [me] these bundles of notes and [then] rest in the car yourself. You have to give service just like a *kulī* (laborer) before me, then I'll be satisfied with you." I told them that. So I want that kind of service. I don't want money from people. I don't want things from people.

Tat dīkṣākrama yogena śāstrārthaṁ vettyasau tataḥ, *tat dīkṣā krama yogena*, then he will initiate you when he is satisfied. The service, what he wants from you, you have to do that service. *Śāstrārthaṁ vettyasau*, [then] he becomes elevated, the disciple becomes elevated. *Abhiṣekaṁ samāsādhya*, then he gets his *abhiṣeka* (*abhiṣeka* means, full prayer with *aśarvad*, with his blessings). *Yo bhavet*, and he becomes a master, that disciple becomes a master afterwards by getting that initiation from [his master] by serving him. *Sa tu kalpita*, although he is a *kalpita* master,...*

A *kalpita* master means, he is a made-master, he is not an automatic master. Some masters in this world take place by the grace of God. They don't need to go to some master for initiation (inaudible). They are blessed from God directly. Those are *akalpita* (*akalpita* means, born-masters, born-masters from God). They have no need to go to a master for initiation for getting elevated. Those are *akalpitas*. He is a *kalpita*, he is made by a master. He is made a master by a master. Do you understand?

*...although he is made, he is *kalpita*, *aśeṣā pāśaugha-vinivartanakovidaḥ*, he can remove all the ignorance from his disciples, whomever may come to him for help.

Wisdom Verses 2 (18:25)

SAMADHĀNAṀ VINĀ ŚĀSTRĀṆAṀ VAIYARTHYAM

SCRIPTURES ARE USELESS WITHOUT PRACTICE

संसारमोहनाशाय शब्दबोधो नहि क्षमः ।
न निवर्तेत तिमिरं कदाचिद्दीपवर्तया ॥२२॥

saṁsāramohanāśāya śabdabodho nahi kṣamaḥ /
na nivarteta timiraṁ kadāciddīpavartayā //22//

The studying of *śāstras* (scriptures) is not capable of removing the illusion that is existing in the world. *Śāstras* will never remove that illusion of *saṁsāra* from your mind. So *śāstras* are useless. If you study *śāstras* only without putting the practical shape there, [then] studying these *śāstras* is useless. *Na nivarteta timira*–he gives an example for that–*timiraṁ* (this darkness) cannot be removed when we give the definition and qualification, describe the qualifications of a candle. This is the qualification of a candle: "a candle can remove all darkness." By these talks, the darkness cannot be removed. Darkness can only be removed when the candle is lit–then darkness will be removed. Otherwise, in the same way, if you go on studying *śāstras* without giving its practical shape, *śāstras* will do nothing. The negligence and ignorance of *saṁsāra* is not removed by *śāstras*.

But there is a doubt now, a doubt can arise in aspirants: When *śāstras* are not capable of removing the darkness of *saṁsāra*, illusion, what for are *śāstras* in this scene? Why old ancient scholars have given the importance of studying *śāstras* then? For that he says another *śloka*:

Wisdom Verses 2 (21:56)

अभ्यस्य वेदशास्त्राणि सारं ज्ञात्वाथबुद्धिमान् ।
पलालमिव धान्यार्थे त्यजेच्छास्त्रमशेषतः ॥२३॥

abhyasya vedaśāstrāṇi sāraṁ jñātvātha buddhimān /
palālamiva dhānyārthe tyajecchāstramaśeṣataḥ //23//

Veda śāstrāṇi, all *śāstra*s should be studied, you should study *śāstra*s, and after studying *śāstra*s wholeheartedly with one-pointedness, *sāraṁ jñā-*, the wise aspirant should extract the essence of the *śāstra*s, what is the background of the *śāstra*s. Only studying is not the end of *śāstra*s–studying. Wise aspirants should take out the essence of *śāstra*s, what is the essence of *śāstra*s. The essence of *śāstra*s is to realize your own Self, to realize the Self of God consciousness. Then once you have realized the Self of God consciousness, *palālam iva dhānyārthe*, just as farmers collect [rice] paddy from the *shali* fields, they collect the paddy along with this grass, and collect it and keep it safely in one pile, and at the time of thrashing, when they thrash it, they take out that paddy out of the grass and then they remove the grass on one side and they throw it away from the paddy, in the same way, you should study the *śāstra*s. When you have found the essence of *śāstra*s, after finding the essence of *śāstra*s, you should leave *śāstra*s for good, you should not study any more *śāstra*s. Go on contemplating on your own nature. This is the purpose of studying *śāstra*s. This is not the end [that for] all your life you should study *śāstra*s and do nothing. This is what he means in this *śloka*.

Wisdom Verses 2 (25:07)

षट्दर्शनमहाकूपे पतिताः पशवः प्रिये ।
न जानन्ति परं तत्त्वं दर्वी पाकरसं यथा ॥२४॥

ṣaṭ darśanamahākūpe patitāḥ paśavaḥ priye /
na jānanti paraṁ tattvaṁ darvī pākarasaṁ yathā //24//

[Lord Śiva]: O dear Pārvatī, *ṣaṭ darśanamahākūpe*, in the well of the six *darśana*s (schools),...*

Right from Śaivism to Nyāya, Vaiśeśika, Vedānta, grammar, and all these, there are supposed to be six sections of *śāstra*s, six schools of *śāstra*s. These six schools of *śāstra*s are actually six wells, deep wells. You know "wells"?

DENISE: Where you get water from.

SWAMIJI: Yes.

*...*ṣaṭ darśana mahākūpe*, in these great and fearful wells, *paśavaḥ*, those who are ignorant persons, they fall and die, they cannot be elevated by going in the depth of those wells. *Na jānanti paraṁ tattvaṁ*, they don't understand, they don't realize the nature which is meant by all these *śāstra*s. The nature of your own Self, they don't realize that [although] they go in the depth of *śāstra*s, the details–those who are ignorant persons. He gives an example: just like *darvi* (*darvi* means, a spoon, a big spoon), when you stir all the vegetables and dishes with that spoon and distribute amongst your guests those delicious dishes with this spoon, but the spoon itself has not tasted anything–this spoon. Although the spoon is involved in each and every action of this, [serving] delicious dishes, but the spoon itself does not experience any taste of this, out of it. In the same way, those ignorant persons, who are given only to *śāstra*s without going in the depth of its purpose–What is the purpose of *śāstra*s? The purpose of *śāstra*s is to realize God–and they don't realize God, they only go on reciting *śloka*s. What is the purpose of that? They won't achieve anything from reciting only. You have to find out the truth which is lying behind it.

Bas, this section is finished. Now there is a section for masters when they find a disqualification of their disciples although they were once graced by their *śaktipāta*. *Śaktipāta* is already inserted in the minds of those disciples, and after sometime, after some period, by his continuous activity, the master understands the crookedness of his behavior.

Wisdom Verses 2 (29:28)

Kadā Guruḥ Śiṣyahṛdayajjñānāharaṇaṁ Kuryāt
When a Master Should Extract a Disciple's Spiritual Knowledge

यदा तु वैचित्र्यवशाज्जानीयात्तस्य तादृशम् ।
विपरीतप्तवृतित्त्वं ज्ञानं तस्मादुपाहरेत् ॥२५॥

yadā tu vaicitryavaśājjānīyāttasya tādṛśam /
viparītaptavṛtittvaṁ jñānaṁ tasmādupāharet //25//

Yadā tu, when, *vaicitryavaśāt* (*vaicitryavaśāt* means, by many actions and behaviors), marking the point of his behavior,...*

Whose behavior?

DENISE: The disciple's.

SWAMIJI: The disciple's behavior, misbehavior he marks. In the beginning, when he initiated him, he marked no misbehavior in his actions. Afterwards, *vaicitryavaśāt*, he misbehaved in such a way that the master became angry with him.

*...*yadā tu*, when, *vaicitryavaśāt*, by his constant misbehavior, *jānīyāt*, he comes to this misunderstanding, the master comes to this understanding that, "He was not worthy to have this *anugraha* (grace) from me, from this initiation. I have initiated him [but] he was not supposed to be initiated by me. He was not capable of this initiation but I have initiated him." And when he sees his misbehavior, *jñānaṁ tasmādupāharet*–there is still time to mend–*jñānaṁ tasmād-upāharet*, you should extract all the knowledge which you had given him, not book knowledge, [but] this spiritual knowledge. Spiritual knowledge you should extract from his mind at once. Keep only worldly knowledge, book knowledge in him, *bas*.

Wisdom Verses 2 (32:12)

तं च त्यजेत्पापवृत्तिं भवेत्तु ज्ञानतत्परः ॥२५-१/२॥

taṁ ca tyajetpāpavṛttiṁ bhavettu jñānatatparaḥ //25b//

Then, you should not keep him in your vicinity. That disciple should be discarded, discarded or kept like outsiders. You should think that he is an outsider. *Bhavettu jñāna tatparaḥ*, and you should never deliver a talk of spirituality in his presence. You must not say anything to him regarding spirituality. And *bhavettu jñāna tatparaḥ*, whenever you see him in front of you, you should close your eyes and keep meditating on your own nature. Don't think of him any more.

Bas, this section is finished in one *śloka* and one half *śloka*. I have recited this.

JOHN: Yes. These are all from the *Tantrāloka*, is it?

SWAMIJI: Yes. But in the *Tantrāloka* he has afterwards said, explained that, "My masters are not in favor of doing this cruel activity for those disciples." Abhinavagupta says, "But I am against it." Abhinavagupta says, "I am against it, I want to do this cruelty for this disciple."

JOHN: He wants to.

SWAMIJI: He wants to, but his masters would like, would prefer not to conduct this kind of cruelty on him. Because [they say], "God will give him punishment in His own way. Why to get involved in this way so that you lose your temper uselessly for him. You should not lose your temper. Leave it to God. God will punish him."

JOHN: That's what the masters said.

SWAMIJI: The masters say, but Abhinavagupta does not agree (laughs).

DENISE: He says do it! (laughs)

SWAMIJI: Yes. He says, "No, I would prefer to do it at that very moment, extract everything and put him to task."

DENISE: Spiritual exile.

SWAMIJI: Yes.

JOHN: That's what Swami Rām did to that one…

SWAMIJI: To one disciple.

JOHN: Because that disciple showed ego, is it?

SWAMIJI: His name was Rām Sodhargar. He was entangled in *māyā* afterwards, he couldn't do anything.

JOHN: Before he had some realization–before that?

SWAMIJI: Oh, he was great, he was a great teacher. He wouldn't care for his wife, he wouldn't care for his children. If they fell from the window from the third story, he wouldn't mind, he wouldn't mind. Then afterwards, [if his child] would come and crawl [near] the window, he would catch hold while delivering lectures. He would keep lectures there and take care of his kids. This happened to him afterwards.

DENISE: He became worried about all his worldly concerns.

SWAMIJI: Yes.[8]

JOHN: And Swami Rām extracted this spiritual realization because he was getting an ego?

SWAMIJI: Swami Rām told him, "You won't get spoiled, you'll earn money by giving lectures, but the spirituality is gone forever from your..."

JOHN: For all lifetimes or this lifetime?

---

8. As Lord Kṛṣṇa explains in the *Bhagavad Gītā*, real knowledge manifests as "*Asaktir*, absolute detachment for everything; *anabhuṣvaṅgaḥ putra dāra gṛhādiṣu*, detachment for son, for wife, and for houses, etcetera." Swamiji explains, "If you have a child, don't leave it to the dogs. Take care of him but don't be attached to it. If that child dies, unfortunately if that child dies, don't get mad. Say that, "It was His doing." Be attached to Him [and be detached] to him. It is to be done, it is to be conducted in the beginning, it is a must." *Bhagavad Gītā* 13.10 audio (LJA archive, 1978). "While feeding [your child] also, you must merge in that God consciousness. That is the real way of Śaivism." *Stava Cintāmaṇi* (LJA archive). "This is the acceptance of *oṁ*, when you believe that you are feeding [your child, but] you are not feeding him for the sake of [him]. *Tat* means, I am feeding [my child] for the sake of *tat*, not for the sake of [him]. *Tat* means "that". Which that? *Sat*, who is existing, who is only existing. Śiva is only existing everywhere and that you have to believe, that you have to know. That is what he says: *tat iti anabhisandhāya phalaṁ*, this fruit of feeding [your child], discard that. I am not feeding [my child], I mean, so he will grow and he will be nourished. I am not nourishing [my child], I am nourishing Lord Śiva. Which Lord Śiva? Who is *sat*. *Sat* means, who is existing, who is only existing. None is existing, nobody else is existing, everywhere." *Bhagavad Gītā* 17.25 audio (LJA archive, 1978).

SWAMIJI: All lifetime.

DENISE: What did he do to deserve that? What wrong did he do?

SWAMIJI: He wouldn't go to study before [Swami] Rām. Because these disciples mislead their master.

DENISE: So the master can be fooled by disciples in that way?

SWAMIJI: Yes, if he is just a fool. They flattered him, flattered Rām Sodhargar and told him…he was witty, more witty than Swami Rām. Swami Rām couldn't explain those things which he did to the disciples. So disciples told him, hinted that he was more than his master. And he accepted that, "I am more than my master." (laughs)

DENISE: "Yes, you're right, I'm greater."

SWAMIJI: He was finished, at once, for good.

JOHN: Did you ever meet that man?

SWAMIJI: Yes, he was living…

JOHN: When you were a boy?

SWAMIJI: Yes, when I was a child, yes.

DENISE: Was he sad?

JOHN: Was he sad afterwards?

SWAMIJI: He was depressed. He was entangled in his own way in household affairs. Afterwards, he kept all the books in the almirah. He was not studying or delivering lectures to anybody.

DENISE: Because it had no more taste any more.

SWAMIJI: No (affirmative), he lost the taste.

JOHN: And this is for all lifetimes or only this lifetime?

SWAMIJI: I don't know what happened to him.

JOHN: But this lifetime was definitely a problem.

SWAMIJI:

Wisdom Verses 2 (38:56)

यदा किञ्चिज्ज्ञोऽहं द्विप इव मदान्धः समभवम् ।
तदा सर्वज्ञोऽस्मीत्यभवदवलिप्तं मम मनः ॥२६॥
यदा किञ्चित् किञ्चिद् बुधजनसकाशादवगतम् ।
तदा मूर्खोऽस्मीति ज्वर इवमदो मे व्यपगतः ॥२७॥

yadā kiñcijjño'haṁ dvipa iva madāndhaḥ samabhavam /
tadā sarvajño'smītyabhavadavaliptaṁ mama manaḥ //26//
yadā kiñcitkiñcidbudhajanasakāśādavagatam /
tadā mūrkho'smīti jvara ivamado me vyapagataḥ //27//

This is the next *śloka*. Because this is the *śloka* which explains that although you understand that you have understood everything of the *śāstra*s, you should think that you have to understand some more points yet. You should not go in this fancy that, "I have understood everything." Although you have understood everything, but still you should not believe that you have understood everything. There is yet to be learned in this world. Some greater scholar will tell you more things which you never had in your lifetime experienced.

So when *kiñcit jño'haṁ*, when I realized some things, some points of spirituality, when I began to realize some points of spirituality, *dvipa iva madāndhaḥ samabhavam*, just like a wild elephant I became wild in society and I kicked all wise people aside and told them, "You are just duffers." I was drowned and soaked in ego that, "I have studied and I am experienced in the *śāstra*s. I am the greatest scholar." When I began to realize some points of *śāstra*s, then this happened to me. I realized that I had known everything. *Dvipa iva madāndhaḥ samabhavam, tadā sarvajño asmi*, then I realized that I have understood everything of the *śāstra*s, *tyabhavat avaliptaṁ mama manaḥ*, and my mind became soaked in this ego that, "I am the topmost wise person in this world." And when *kiñcit kiñcit*, some points I heard from the lips of great scholars, when I realized it in its true sense the important points from the lips of great scholars, and at that moment I realized that I was just a duffer, [that] I have realized nothing. And this *jvara iva*, this *jvara* (fever) of the ego (*jvara* means the temperature of the ego) went down below from 110 to zero. This temperature at once came down and I found that I had realized nothing when I began to realize some points from the lips of great masters.

This is the *śloka* that you should keep in view. You should never think that, "I am studying Śaivism and I know Śaivism." You should never think that. You should think that, "I am just trying to understand Śaivism." This way, you will realize something. Otherwise, if you think that you have realized [everything], it will be just the ego and it will sentence you to the lower scale of disability for good.

Wisdom Verses 2 (40:06)

Patiśivaśabdayoḥ Nirvacanam
Nominating Śiva as "Pati"

शासनरोधनपालनपाचनयोगात्स सर्वमुपकुरुते ।
तेन पतिः श्रेयोमय एव शिवो नाशिवं किमपि तत्र ॥२८॥

śāsanarodhanapālanapācanayogātsa sarvamupakurute /
tena patiḥ śreyomaya eva śivo nāśivaṁ kimapi tatra //28//

Śiva is actually *pati* (*pati* means, husband of the whole universe). He is the husband of the whole universe, and He is Śiva, He is called Śiva. He actually *sarvam upakurute*, He elevates each and every individual who are created by Him in this field of the universe. In this field of the universe, whoever is created by Lord Śiva, He elevates him, He goes on elevating them. But there are so many ways to elevate. *Śāsana*, by *śāsana*, by putting him to task, He elevates him. When he is mislead in *saṁsāra*, he is doing some mischievous actions, when he commits mischievous actions, by putting *śāsana* on him, discipline, and punishing him, He gives him punishment. Who?

DEVOTEES: Lord Śiva.

SWAMIJI: Lord Śiva. Punishment for what? Just to elevate him, just to elevate him. That is *śāsana*. *Rodhana*; *rodhana* means, when he is stuck in some misbehavior, doing misbehaving actions continuously and he is stuck somewhere and he doesn't go up or down, he is stuck there, Lord Śiva [makes] him to stay there in a stuck position just to give him some punishment, threatening that, "You will never come out of this," so that he will, in the next few lives or in the [coming] future in his [present] life, he'll be cautious in behaving. That is *rodhana*. *Śāsana* is giving that punishment. *Rodhana* is…

DENISE: Being stuck in one position.

SWAMIJI:…just let him remain stuck in his own way and not get out of that gap. And *pālana*; *pālana* means, one who recites His name wholeheartedly with great devotion, with great love, He keeps him in

His lap and kisses him, gives him a hug. This is also one way of elevating him. This is the nearest way to elevate. The one who behaves like this…behaves like what?

DENISE: He keeps him in His lap and gives him hugs…

SWAMIJI: No, the the one, the aspirant, who behaves like that, then He keeps him in His lap and hugs him and protects him from all sides. Those also He protects, those [who misbehave]. *Rodhana*, *pālana*, and *pācanayogāt*; *pācanayogāt* means, [by ripening the fruit of actions]. Some do actions but not so wholeheartedly, they do actions but the result does not come soon, so they are waiting for that result [and wonder], "Why that result has not come? Am I not doing wholeheartedly this action?" *Pācana*, He elevates him by *pācana*, by ripening his actions, activities. It takes time in him; unless it is ripe, the fruit does not come, this fruit is not revealed to him. So it comes in time. So he should not get worried about it. Lord Śiva elevates everybody! He is bent upon doing this thing. *Tena patiḥ*, this way, He is supposed to be the husband of the universe. *Śreyomayaḥ eva śiva*, and He is supposed to be Śiva (Śiva means, all-around protecting element). *Nāśivam kimapi tatra*, the negation of protection is not born there in the kingdom of Lord Śiva. The negation of that…what?

JOHN: Protection.

SWAMIJI: Protection. Protection is never ignored there.

Wisdom Verses 2 (50:40)

ईदृग्रूपं कियदपि रुद्रोपेन्द्रादिषु स्फुरेद्येनः ।
तेनावच्छेदनुदे परममहत्पदविशेषणमुपातम् ॥२९॥

īdṛgrūpaṁ kiyadapi rudropendrādiṣu sphuredyenaḥ /
tenāvacchedanude paramamahatpadaviśeṣaṇamupātam //29//

Īdṛgrūpaṁ kiyat api, this formation of being a husband (*pati*) or being Śiva of the universe, *pati* can be nominated your physical husband also, Śiva can be nominated your father also. Your father could be nominated as Śiva, your mother could be nominated as Pārvatī, but that Pārvatī and that Śiva–[your mother] is Pārvatī, there is no doubt about it; or [your father] is Śiva–but we have, in the *Tantrāloka*, [Abhinavagupta] has put in place of *"pati,"* *"mahāpati"* (great husband), and in place of "Śiva" he has put "Paramaśiva." Paramaśiva means, Paramaśiva is only Lord Śiva. ["Śiva" means], Śiva or everybody. Śiva can be your father, Śiva can be some respected being, Śiva can be your officer, but Paramaśiva is only one, that is Lord Śiva. In the same way, *pati* (husband), there are so many husbands in this world, but *mahāpati* is only Lord Śiva. *Tena avacchedanude*, this *avaccheda*, this limitation, to ignore this limitation of being *pati* or being Śiva, you have [to] put these [adjectives], *param* and *mahat*: *paramapati* and *mahāpati*, Paramaśiva and Mahāśiva. These [adjectives] are put, adjusted with that Paramaśiva.

Do you understand?

Wisdom Verses 2 (53:50) end
Wisdom Verses 3 (00:11) start

Mahābhairavadeva Śabdasya Nirvacanam
The Explanatioin of "Mahābhairava Deva"

देवो ह्यन्वर्थशास्त्रोक्तैः शब्दैः समुपदिश्यते ।
महाभैरवदेवोऽयं पतिर्यः परमः शिवः ॥३०॥

devo hyanvarthaśāstroktaiḥ śabdaiḥ samupadiśyate /
mahābhairavadevo'yaṁ patiryaḥ paramaḥ śivaḥ //30//

This *devatā*, this *deva* (God), *anvarthaśāstroktaiḥ śabdaiḥ*, by the *śabda*s (words) which are derived from the *śāstra*s and grammars, by those *śabda*s, this *deva* is being explained. The formation of *deva*, the actual position of *deva*, is explained by *śāstra*s and by the statement of grammars.

Mahābhairava *deva*, Mahābhairava *deva*, supreme Bhairava *deva*, He is called "supreme Bhairava *deva*," otherwise your father can be Bhairava. But Lord Śiva is Mahābhairava. Your mother can be Bhairavī, but Pārvatī will be Mahābhairavī. So these qualifications are adjusted, added to that Bhairava to discriminate the position of Bhairava from other Bhairavas. *Avacchedanude*, this limitation is negated from that Bhairava, that supreme Bhairava, so *parama* and *mahat*, these qualifications are added in that name of Bhairava.

Now he gives the definition of Bhairava:

Wisdom Verses 3 (02:14)

BHAIRAVA ŚABDASYA NIRVACANAM
THE EXPLANATION OF "BHAIRAVA"

विश्वं बिभर्ति पूरणधारणयोगेन तेन च भ्रियते ॥३१॥
सविमर्शतया रवरूपतश्च संसार भीरुहितकृच्च ॥३२॥

viśvaṁ bibharti pūraṇadhāraṇayogena tena ca bhriyate //31a//
savimarśatayā ravarūpataśca saṁsāra bhīruhitakṛcca //32a//
(only the first line of each verse is presented)[9]

Viśvaṁ bibharti, (He) who protects this whole universe is Bhairava. How He protects this universe? *Pūraṇa dhāraṇa yogena*, He fills it, all gaps are filled in this universe by Bhairava. Where there is a lacking of something, it is filled with that element. So, this whole universe becomes full, it possesses the fullness just like Bhairava, and that fullness is derived from Bhairava in this universe. *Tena ca bhriyate*, this universe also produces fullness *for* Bhairava, the universe also creates fullness for Bhairava. Bhairava creates fullness for the universe; the universe creates fullness for Bhairava. So these two elements, Bhairava and the universe, are actually one in its right manner. Why they are one? This universe is the embodiment of His energy (*śakti*), and Bhairava is the embodiment of Śiva. Bhairava is Śiva and the universe is Śakti. It is well said in Śaivism:

9. See Appendix for complete verses.

śaktayo'sya jagatkṛtsnaṁ śaktimāṁstu maheśvaraḥ /[10]

All His energies are established in the establishment of the universe. The universe is the combination of all energies, all energies of Lord Śiva, and the energy-holder is Śiva. This is Bhairava. Bhairava is that being who fills the gap in the universe and whose gap is filled by the universe (whose some gaps are filled by the universe). The universe fills some gaps [in Bhairava] and Bhairava fills gaps in the universe–and the universe fills gaps in Bhairava. Actually, these two elements are one. One is the embodiment of Śakti and another is the embodiment of Śiva. *Savimarśatayā ravarūpataśca*–Bhairava is not only this–Bhairava is also that being who creates just like a loud-speaker, who creates the loud-speaking element in your nature for asking the help of Lord Śiva at the time of torture, being tortured or trodden down. When you are trodden down, you cry, you cry and ask His…

DENISE: Mercy.

SWAMIJI:…mercy in that. And that mercy, the abode of mercy is Bhairava, from whom this mercy is produced for you. That is *savimarśatayā ravarūpataśca*. And *saṁsāra bhīru hitakṛt ca*–He is Bhairava–and *saṁsāra bhīru*, who is terrified, who is all-round terrified by the actual position of this world,…*

Because the world is…sometime it seems a terrifying element for everybody, it terrifies. That thing happens which is not (laughs) just thought over, that it would be true.

DENISE: The unimaginable.

SWAMIJI: Yes. So it is terrifying.

*…and those people who are terrified of this *saṁsāra*, *hitakṛt ca*, He gives him some relief by reciting His name. One who is absolutely caught in that cycle of torture, at some fearful occasion he takes refuge in Lord Śiva and He gives him some satisfaction, some relief. He consoles his nature: "Oh, it is like this happening, you cannot cure it, it is incurable."

Wisdom Verses 3 (08:37)

10. Quote from the *Sarvamaṅgalā Śāstra*. See *Tantrāloka* 5.40.

संसारभीतिजनितात्द्रवात्परामर्शतोऽपि हृदि जातः ॥३३॥
प्रकटीभूतं भवभयविमर्शनं शक्तिपाततो येन ॥३४॥

saṁsārabhītijanitādravātparāmarśato'pi hṛdi jātaḥ //33a//
prakaṭībhūtaṁ bhavabhayavimarśanaṁ śaktipātato yena //34a//
(only the first line of each verse is presented)[11]

Saṁsāra bhīti janitāt ravāt, when the *bhīti* (the *bhīti* means, the greatest fear) rises from this world, *saṁsāra bhīti janitāt*, and at that time when you see some disaster, some floods, and in those floods everybody is drowned–this kind of disaster also takes place in this world, you experience this–or a terrible earthquake kills millions of people in one second–these kinds of disasters–*saṁsāra bhīti janitāt*, by the fearful act in *saṁsāra*, *ravāt*, and that cry of the people, *parāmarśato'pi hṛdi jātaḥ*, when by crying, crying repeatedly, crying again and again, He gives consolation in your heart, in the heart of those who are caught in this torture. That is Bhairava who gives consolation at that moment. *Prakaṭī bhūtaṁ bhavabhayavimarśanaṁ śaktipātato yena*, by His *śaktipāta* (grace), the *bhaya vimarśanaṁ*, this analyzing of this, what is this fear, wherefrom this fear has risen, by going in the depth to find out what is the reason of this fear, the reason just comes in his view, in his nature, by the *śaktipāta* of Lord Śiva, that it is the way of the universe, you should not worry about it.

Wisdom Verses 3 (11:53)

नक्षत्रप्रेरककालतत्त्वसंशोषकारिणो ये च ।
कालग्रासममाधानरसिकमनःसु तेषु च प्रकटः ॥३५॥

nakṣatraprerakakālatattvasaṁśoṣakāriṇo ye ca /
kālagrāsasamādhānarasikamanaḥsu teṣu ca prakaṭaḥ //35//

---

11. See Appendix for complete verses.

Another definition of Bhairava he gives in this *śloka*.

Those (*ye ca*, and those) who are destroying the being of the lord of death, who destroy the being of the lord of death, who are bent upon destroying the lord of death who is *nakṣatra prerakakāla tattva*, who is governing on the position of all these planets, the lord of death who is governing all the positions of all the planets which are governing this whole universe,...*

And the lord of death governs those planets to see that everything is going on all right and everybody dies in time.

JOHN: *Kāla tattva* is the lord of death?

SWAMIJI: Lord of death, yes.

*...*saṁśoṣakāriṇo*, who destroy those, who are the destroyer of *kāla tattva*,...*

JOHN: *Kāla tattva* is time.

SWAMIJI: *Kāla tattva* means, the lord of death. Time is death because when there is time, the existence of time in this universe, [there is death]. If there was no time, there [would be] no death. As long as time is alive, death is alive. Because time goes on, time slips [away] and there will be death in the end.

*...but those who are bent upon destroying this ruler of time (that is, the lord of death), those, who are those? *Kāla grāsa samādhāna rasikamanaḥsu*, they are happy to digest in their own nature, in nothingness, the position of the lord of death. They just eat the lord of death, they just finish the lord of death, and they are bent upon finishing that lord of death. Who are they? Those are yogis. *Teṣu ca prakaṭaḥ*, those yogis, the one who is seen by, who is experienced by those yogis who are bent upon destroying the lord of death who is governing on all the planets of the world, those yogis are bent upon destroying the lord of death, for those, [the one] who is available, who is available at all times,...*

[For] whom?

JOHN: Parabhairava.

SWAMIJI: Those yogis who are bent upon destroying the position of the lord of death.

*...the one who is available to them all times is Bhairava. So Bhairava is side-by-side existing. To whom?

JOHN: Those yogis.

SWAMIJI: To yogis.

DENISE: Those yogis who have destroyed the lord of death.

SWAMIJI: Yes. This is one definition, another definition of Bhairava. Now he says another definition:

Wisdom Verses 3 (16:27)

सङ्कोचिपशुजनभिये यासां रवणं स्वकरणदेवीनाम् ।
अन्तर्बहिश्चतुर्विधखेचर्यादिकगणस्यापि ॥३६॥
तस्य स्वामी संसारवृत्तिविघट्टनमहाभीमः ।
भैरव इति गुरुभिरिमैरन्वर्थैः संस्तुतः शास्त्रे ॥३७॥
(कुलकं)

saṅkocipaśujanabhiye yāsāṁ ravaṇaṁ svakaraṇadevīnām /
antarbahiścaturvidhakhecaryādikagaṇasyāpi //36//
tasya svāmī saṁsāravṛttivighaṭṭanamahābhīmaḥ /
bhairava iti gurubhirimairanvarthaiḥ saṁstutaḥ śāstre //37//

Saṅkoci paśu janabhiye, those who are governing all the organs of individuals,…*

Which organs? The cognitive organs and the organs of action, the *karmendriya* and *jñānendriya* of every individual. Every individual has got these ten organs, and it is shrunken, these organs are shrunken in their own way in individuals, in each and every individual.

*…*yāsāṁ ravaṇaṁ svakaraṇa devīnām*, those who are attentive to those organs, who are governing those organs one-by-one,…*

For instance, there is the organ of seeing, there is the organ of touching, there is the organ of smelling, there is the organ of hearing, there is the organ of tasting, there is the organ of sex. All these organs have in their own way their gods who are governing those.

JOHN: Those *śakti*s. "Gods" means, *śakti*s (energies)?

SWAMIJI: Yes. Those are *khecarī*, *gocarī*, *dikcarī*, and *bhūcarī*, these four *śakti*s.[12] They are produced by God for governing all these organs [so] that the activity of these organs should be done, should be experienced properly. [In this way], if you see with the eyes something, if you see something for sex, it gives a sensation in the sexual organ–by seeing. So, this connecting-rod is connected by those…

JOHN: *Śakti*s.

SWAMIJI:…four *śakti*s: *khecarī, gocarī, dikcarī,* and *bhūcarī.* So they are taking care of all this.

JOHN: So it's the same thing when you smell something tasty, you get the urge for eating. Is that the same kind of connection like that?

DENISE: When you see *achar* (pickles), your mouth waters?

SWAMIJI: Yes, the mouth waters. But it goes, the connecting-rod is that *śakti.*

DENISE: *Śakti.* But it seems automatic.

SWAMIJI: It is automatic, it doesn't take any time to pass on, to pass on from one place to another place. For instance, you see something, with the eyes you see *aloo bhukara* (plum) fruit, it gives you taste in [your mouth], and the teeth water. But from the eyes, how has it reached in your teeth and you want to eat it (laughs)? So this conducting union is done by these *śakti*s.

**…antarbahi*, it is *antar* (inside) and *bahi* (outside) also, *tasya svāmī*, who governs all this in a collective way is Bhairava. And Bhairava is He also, *saṁsāra vṛtti vighaṭṭana mahābhīmaḥ*, who is fearful, who has become fearful–not in a bad sense, He is not fearful in a bad sense; Bhairava, Bhairava is not fearful–Bhairava is fearful in this sense that He destroys the position of ignorance. For ignorance, He is fearfull. He eats and dissolves ignorance in His own nature. So, ignorance does not remain at all before Him. For that, He is *bhīma* (fearful)…

JOHN: Ignorance means, limitation?

SWAMIJI:…to destroy ignorance. Limitation, yes. *Bhairava iti*

---

12. "*Khecarī* is those cycle of energies which reside in the cycle of voidness. *Gocarī* is the cycle of energies that resides in this organs of cognition. *Dikcarī* means those energies which reside in the organs of action. *Bhūcarī* are the energies which reside in the outside world. In all these cycles you find only the kingdom of *khecarī*." *Parātrīśikā Vivaraṇa* (LJA archive).

gurubhirimair anvarthaiḥ saṁstutaḥ śāstre. Look, Abhinavagupta has committed a mistake in the *Tantrāloka*, a grammatical mistake. "*Imaiḥ*" is not correct in grammar–"*imaiḥ*." In place of "*imaiḥ*," he ought to have put "*ebiḥ*"; "*ebiḥ*" is the correct word for "*imaiḥ*."

Imaiḥ anvarthaiḥ, by these explanations which we have done beforehand, these explanations of Bhairava, Bhairava is explained in these explanations which we have already done (these explanations, *imaiḥ*).[13] "*Imaiḥ*" is incorrect; "*imaiḥ*" means, these, by these explanations. But from a grammatical point of view, "*imaiḥ*" is incorrect. In place of "*imaiḥ*," he ought to have put this word "*ebiḥ*"–in place of "*imaiḥ*." "*Imaiḥ*" is incorrect from the grammatical way. But no *ācāraya* (teacher) had the guts to correct his mistake. So, the commentator of the *Tantrāloka* says, at the time of commenting upon this "*imaiḥ*" word of Abhinavagupta, he says, "*imaiḥ* means, *ebiḥ*."

DENISE: He didn't change it.

SWAMIJI: He didn't change this word.

Wisdom Verses 3 (23:50)

Viśvaikarūpaviśvātma viśvasargādi kāraṇam…"*viśvātman*" is incorrect.

JOHN: Yes.

SWAMIJI:

विश्वैकरूपविश्वात्म विश्वसर्गादिकारणम् ।
परप्रकाशवपुषं स्तुमः स्वच्छन्दभैरवम् ॥ ३८ ॥

viśvaikarūpaviśvātma viśvasargādi kāraṇam /
paraprakāśavapuṣaṁ stumaḥ svacchandabhairavam //38//

13. Swamiji's translation of this verse is as follows: "In that *Śivatanu Śāstra*, in that *śāstra* which is nominated as *Śivatanu*, our masters have explained in this way the reality of Bhairava." *Tantrāloka* 1.99 (LJA archive).

We bow at the feet of that Svacchandanātha with five heads (Īśāna, Tapuruṣa, Sadyojāta, Vāmadeva, and Aghora, these five mouths). Who possesses these five mouths, that Svacchandanātha, we bow before Him. We bow our heads before that Svacchandanātha, who is *viśvaika rūpa*, who is one with this whole universe, who is universal, *viśvātma*, who is the embodiment of the universe, *viśvasargādi kāraṇam*, who creates the universe, who protects the universe, and who destroys the universe, who reveals the universe, who conceals the universe with His five acts (creation, protection, destruction, concealing, and revealing). *Para prakāśa vapuṣaṁ*, and that Svacchanda Bhairava is *para prakāśa vapuṣaṁ*, the embodiment of supreme light, the light beyond all the three lights. It is above all the three lights. These three lights are seen and experienced in this universe: one light of *agni* (fire), one light of the moon, and another light of the sun. All these three, He supersedes their light. That light is beyond these three lights. It is not the light of *agni* (that is, subjective light), it is not subjective light. It is not the light of the sun (that is, cognitive light), it is not cognitive light. And it is not objective light (that is, of the moon). It is neither of the object, neither from cognition, nor from the subject. It is beyond these three *pramātṛ bhava*s.

JOHN: *Pramiti*?

SWAMIJI: This is *pramiti*, yes, *pramiti*. [Kashmiri:] He knows this theory.[14]

Wisdom Verses 3 (27:08:46)

मध्यप्राणनिविष्टहंसपरमः यो रोमकूपाश्रयः ।
प्राणः सूक्ष्मविमर्शशालिवपुषः सार्धत्रिकोटयात्मकः ॥३९॥
तान्मन्त्रात्मतया विलोमयति यः स्वच्छन्दनाथः परो ।

14. "*Pramiti* is that state where subjective consciousness prevails without the agitation of objectivity. Where the agitation of objectivity is also found in subjective consciousness, that is the state of *pramātṛ*. In other words, when he is residing in his own nature, that subjective consciousness is the state of *pramiti*." *Kashmir Shaivism–The Secret Supreme*, 11.81.

देवोऽसौ विदधातु भैरववपुः तेजः परं शाश्वतम् ॥४०॥

madhyaprāṇaniviṣṭahaṁsa paramaḥ yo romakūpāśrayaḥ /
prāṇaḥ sūkṣmavimarśaśālivapuṣaḥ sārdhatrikoṭayātmakaḥ //39//
tānmantrātmatayā vilomayati yaḥ svacchandanāthaḥ paro /
devo'sau vidadhātu bhairavavapuḥ tejaḥ paraṁ śāśvatam //40//

These two *śloka*s are combined, both in one. In Sanskrit, it is called *yugalakam*. *Yugalakam* means, both *śloka*s are only one sentence.

JOHN: One long meaning, one combined meaning.

SWAMIJI: Yes (Swamiji repeats the first verse). *Madhya prāṇa*, in the central vein of breath, *niviṣṭa haṁsa paramaḥ yo romakūpa āśrayaḥ* (these *romakūpa* means, the well of each hair, the wells of the pores, all the pores), and in these pores, there are special pores. Those are three *crore*s and a half *crore* [in number]. One hundred *lakh*s (100,000) is one *crore* (10 million). Three hundred *lakh*s and fifty *lakh*s.

DENISE: Pores?

SWAMIJI: Pores. Three hundred *lakh*s and fifty *lakh*s.

DENISE: Three and a half *lakh*s?

INDERJI: No, three hundred and fifty *lakh*s.

SWAMIJI: Three hundred and fifty *lakh*s (a half *crore*). Three *crore*s and a half *crore* (35 million), these are [the number of special] pores in the body. And these are the openings of breath produced by *madhyanāḍī* (the central vein), which is residing in *suṣumna nāḍī*. The central vein, *suṣumna*, these pathways are produced from this central vein. How many pathways?

JOHN: Three…

DENISE: Three hundred.

SWAMIJI: Three hundred? Not three hundred (laughs)! Three *crore*s and fifty *lakh*s, these strings, , you must call it "veins." *Madhya prāṇa niviṣṭa haṁsa paramaḥ yo romakūpa āśrayaḥ* means, which are residing in *romakūpa*, each and every *romakūpa*, the openings of all these pores. So, *prāṇa* is actually…although there are only five *prāṇa*s (*prāṇa*, *apāna*, *samāna*, *udāna*, and *vyāna*), but in fact, when you calculate it differentiatedly, these breaths are three *crore*s and fifty *lakh*s breaths, which are produced by the central vein in the body. And these breaths are referred to…in fact, in heaven also, in the upper field, purer creation… one creation is the creative field which is created in the impure way, that is, from earth to *māyā*. From the earth element to the *māyā* element is the impure creative scale, and that resides in one's own body also; and that resides in the whole universe also, in a hundred and eighteen worlds also. And there is one pure creative section–pure. It was impure from earth to *māyā*. And from *māyā* to Sadāśiva…actually, not including *māyā*. *Māyā* will go in the impure field of creation. Above *māyā* there is Śuddhavidyā. Śuddhavidyā is conducted by *mantra pramātṛns*. *Mantra pramātṛns* are those who are residing in Śuddhavidyā, those who are experiencing the state of God consciousness of Śuddhavidyā. This God consciousness also is differently experienced by yogis. One kind of God consciousness, it is inferior God consciousness. It will be experienced in Śuddhavidyā. And another, when you go ahead, another God consciousness is experienced in Īśvara. That is superior to this God consciousness [of Śuddhavidyā]. Another God consciousness is experienced in Sadāśiva. This is superior to that [Īśvara] also. Another God consciousness is experienced in Śiva and Śakti. That is the purest. And the beginning point of pure God consciousness is found in *mantra pramātr bhāva* (*mantra pramātṛ bhāva* means, Śuddhavidyā). And below Śuddhavidyā there are the *vijñānākala*s. *Vijñānākala*s are three *crore*s and fifty *lakh*s. *Vijñānākala pramātṛ*s in heaven, they are three *crore*s and fifty *lakh*s in number. They are residing in heaven.

JOHN: This is *mahāmāyā*?

SWAMIJI: It is in *mahāmāyā*. In *mahāmāyā*, those are residing in *vijñānākala*.

JOHN: In-between *māyā* and Śuddhavidyā.

SWAMIJI: Yes, between *māyā* and Śuddhavidyā there is *vijñānākala*. *Vijñānākala*s are three *crore*s and fifty *lakh*s in number. *Tān mantrātmatayā vilomayati yaḥ*, and Svacchandanātha is conducting this.

Wisdom Verses 3 (35:08)

śuddhe'dhvani śivaḥ kartā
prokto'nanto'site prabhuḥ[15]

---

15. Jayaratha quotes this verse from the *Kiraṇāgama* in his commentary for *Tantrāloka* 8.331.

There are two Śivas. One Śiva takes the formation of Anantabhaṭṭāraka and another Śiva takes the formation of Śiva. The Anantabhaṭṭāraka, [Śiva] who takes the formation of Anantabhaṭṭāraka, he conducts the impure state of the universe, that is, from earth to *māyā*. He is responsible for that–to create it, to protect it, to destroy it, to conceal it, to reveal it. Who?

DISCIPLES: Anantabhaṭṭāraka.

SWAMIJI: Anantabhaṭṭāraka. And for the other section, the pure section, beginning from *vijñānākala*, then *mantra* (Śuddhavidyā), then Īśvara, Sadāśiva, and Śiva, these five, these five pure elements are conducted by Śiva Himself. Śiva is handling all this. And these *vijñānākala pramātṛ*s, who are residing in the *vijñānākala* state (in *mahāmāyā*) experiencing God consciousness, and those are in number three *crore*s and fifty *lakh*s in number. Those three *crore*s and fifty *lakh*s [of] *mantra pramātā*s, in time, they are changed, they are dissolved in Śuddhavidyā (*mantra*) by Lord Śiva. Because this pure state of God consciousness is for elevation, there is no fear of decreasing. On the other hand, it is increasing, it has the tendency to rise. Whereas that, the *aśudhādhva* (*aśudhādhva* means, from earth to *māyā* [16]), it has the tendency to rise and to fall also, it can fall also from…

DENISE: It's unstable, completely unstable.

SWAMIJI: But [the pure section] is not, it has the tendency of rising. So, Lord Śiva handles those, sentences those *vijñānākala pramātṛn*s, [which number] three *crore*s and fifty *lakh*s, in the state of Śuddhavidyā. Then, in the state of Śuddhavidyā, He pushes those in the state of Īśvara, then He pushes those in the state of Sadāśiva, then He pushes those in His lap. So there is the end of the experience of God consciousness in fullness. That Svacchandanātha, we bow to that Svacchandanātha, who does this job in the pure elementary state. This is the meaning of this *śloka*.

JOHN: So what is the connection of these three *crore* and fifty *lakh* [of] *vijñānākalin*s to these three *crore* and fifty *lakh prāṇa*s?

SWAMIJI: Whatever is residing in the universe, that you'll find in your own body. This is the mystery, this is the secret of…"*ekai katrāpi tattve'pi ṣaṭtriṁśattattvarūpatā*," even in one tiny insect, there are

16. Lit., the impure path.

thirty-six elements, there is the power of thirty-six elements–in that mosquito (Swamiji demonstrates), who is sucking blood.

DENISE: And a hundred and eighteen worlds, too?

SWAMIJI: One hundred and eighteen worlds, yes, yes. He has the capacity of going to one hundred and eighteen worlds, he has the capacity of residing in thirty-six elements, he has the capacity of residing in the five *kalās* (*nivṛtti kalā*, *pratiṣṭhā kalā*, *vidyā kalā*, *śāntā kalā*, and *śāntātītā kalā*)–that small tiny insect who can be smashed very easily by us.

SHANNA: If you can catch them.

SWAMIJI: And Svacchandanātha who does this job, we bow before His feet. And that Svacchandanātha, may that Svacchandanātha bestow us that *prakāśa* (light) who is owned by Him always, that *prakāśa* of Lord Śiva.

JOHN: That's *para prakāśa*?

SWAMIJI: *Para prakāśa*, yes.

JOHN: Light of consciousness? *Prakāśa* means here? That *prakāśa* that is owned by Him is what?

SWAMIJI: The light of consciousness, nothing else.

JOHN: But the highest light.

SWAMIJI: The highest light, not this light, not the light of *prameya*, not the light of *pramāṇa*, not the light of *pramātṛ*...

JOHN: *Pramiti bhāva*.

SWAMIJI: *Pramiti bhāva*, yes. But it is very easy for Him to do if He so wills, wishes. For that he says says another *śloka*:

Wisdom Verses 3 (40:39)

दुष्करं सुकरीकर्तुं दुःखं सुखयितुं तथा ।
एकवीरा स्मृतिर्यस्य तं स्मरामः स्मरद्विषम् ॥४१॥

duṣkaraṁ sukarīkartuṁ duḥkhaṁ sukhayituṁ tathā /
ekavīrā smṛtiryasya taṁ smarāmaḥ smaradviṣam //41//

Ekavīrā smṛtiryasya (*ekavīrā smṛti* means, one-time memory), only if you remember Him only once in your life, remember Him wholeheartedly,...*

Remembering is not just to remember Him as routine-like. Routine-like remembrance does not mean anything, it is no remembrance, it is equal to nothing. Not routine-like, you should remember Him, really.

*...if you really remember Him only once in your life, do you know what He does for you? *Duṣkaraṁ sukarīkartuṁ*, He will make the impossible possible (*duṣkaraṁ* means, the impossible). The impossible thing will become possible to you. By what?

DENISE: By remembering Him once.

SWAMIJI: Once in your life. *Duḥkhaṁ sukhayita*, and heaps of pains in this universe will become heaps of joy for you by this remembering Him once in your lifetime, if you remember Him wholeheartedly (*eka-vīrā smṛtiryasya*). *Duṣkaraṁ sukarīkartuṁ*, the impossible becomes possible: *duḥkhaṁ* (pain) takes the formation of joy. *Taṁ smarāmaḥ smaradviṣam*, how great is this news for me. I don't remember Him only once, I remember Him always! What will happen to me? I don't [know]! Something huge may happen to me! It is likely to happen very soon to me because I remember Him always, every now and then, in each and every moment. At each and every moment, I remember Him.

The glory of that remembering Him only once in a lifetime makes the impossible possible, and pain is converted into pleasure, joy. What will happen to him who remembers Him always? And I am that guy who remembers Him [always]. He says that.

DENISE: Abhinavagupta.

SWAMIJI: Yes.[17]

JOHN: Swamiji, in that previous verse (40), what is the meaning of the word "Bhairava" in that last verse? *Devo'sau vida-...*

SWAMIJI: *Devo'sau vidadhātu bhairavavapuḥ*, let that *deva* who is Bhairava and Svacchandanātha, let Him bestow us *tejaḥ param śāśvatam*, that *prakāśa*, that which is established *prakāśa*, and *śāśvatam* (*śāśvatam* means, immortal *prakāśa*, that *prakāśa* which does not go away).

---

17. This verse is from Bhaṭṭanārāyaṇa's *Stava Cintāmaṇi*, verse 82.

Wisdom Verses 3 (44:51)

क्षमः कां नापदं हन्तुं कां दातुं संपदं न वा ।
योऽसौ सो दयितोऽस्माकं देवदेवो वृषध्वजः ॥४२॥

kṣamaḥ kāṁ nāpadaṁ hantuṁ kāṁ dātuṁ saṁpadaṁ na vā /
yo'sau so dayito'smākaṁ devadevo vṛṣadhvajaḥ //42//

That Being, *kṣamaḥ kāṁ nāpadaṁ hantuṁ*, He is capable to destroy each and every tragedy of life; each and every tragedy of life He is capable of destroying in one glance. *Kṣamaḥ* means, He is capable of *kāṁ nāpadaṁ hantuṁ* (all *āpadaṁ* means, tragedy, torture, universal torture), that universal torture which is removed, to remove that universal torture, He is capable of that. The one who is capable of removing for good the torture of the universe, the torture in the universe, and *kāṁ dātuṁ saṁpadaṁ na vā*, and who is capable of bestowing all the pleasures of life to you instantaneously, and that Being–you know who is that Being?–He is our daddy (*dayito asmākaṁ*, He is our daddy), *devadeva*, He is the Lord of lords, and *vṛṣadhvajaḥ*, you will know Him, He has got a flag, and on that flag is the image of a bull. He is our daddy (laughs).

JOHN: Daddy?

SWAMIJI: Daddy.

JOHN: D-a-d-d-y, that daddy? Like our father, huh?

SWAMIJI: Yes. *Kṣamaḥ kāṁ nāpadaṁ hantuṁ kāṁ dātuṁ saṁpadaṁ na vā, yo'sau so dayito'smākaṁ-, dayito* means a lovable daddy, who is never rebuking you, who is always behaving [towards] me with love-full words, love-full behavior–who never rebukes him. And the sign of His flag you'll find the shape of a bull.

Wisdom Verses 3 (48:02) end

Wisdom Verses 4 (00:11) start

Utkrānti Vidhi Kramaḥ
The Master's Procedure for a Dying Disciple

दृष्ट्वा शिष्यं जराग्रस्तं व्याधिभिः परिपीडितम् ।
उत्क्रमय्य ततस्त्वेनं परतत्त्वे नियोजयेत् ॥४३॥
सर्वमप्यथवा भोगं मन्यमानो विरूपकम् ।
उत्क्रमय्य ततस्त्वेनं परतत्त्वे नियोजयेत् ॥४४॥

dṛṣṭvā śiṣyaṁ jarāgrastaṁ vyādhibhiḥ paripīḍitam /
utkramayya tatastvenaṁ paratattve niyojayet //43//
sarvamapyathavā bhogaṁ manyamāno virūpakam /
utkramayya tatastvenaṁ paratattve niyojayet //44//

These *śloka*s are together.

JOHN: Yes, could you sing the first one again please, Sir?

SWAMIJI: (Swamiji repeats the verses) Now, there are two alternatives for a disciple who is going to die, for the disciple of a master who is going to die, or who has lost all curiosity in the universe, [for] universal enjoyments. That is in two ways. One section is those people who are entangled by old age; *vyādhibhiḥ paripīḍitam*, who is entangled and eaten by all kinds of diseases, who is filled with diseases all-round. First, who is absolutely old and who is surrounded by all diseases. This kind of disciple, if he sees, the master, when the master sees this kind of disciple, for him there is no need to wait for him [to die]. *Utkramayya*, you should handle that disciple in such a way: you should extract that soul from that body–there is no fear–you should extract the soul from that body which is fully entangled by all diseases and old age, and *paratattve niyojayet*, you should unite that soul with the point of supreme God consciousness. Then he will die and be connected with that supreme God consciousness. So there will be no repeated births and deaths, they stop for him for good. This is only at the time when you are fed up with your old age and diseases all-round. For him, there is scope. There is this scope that his master will…It is directions for masters, these two *śloka*s are directions for masters, how a master should handle these kind of disciples. One section of disciples is those disciples who are really old enough and who are entangled, who are caught by all diseases, and there is no hope for their recovering in this life. So you make it shorter, the master should make their lives shorter, so they will throw this body at once and he will unite those [disciples] in supreme God consciousness. They will fly in peace.

And there is another section also of this type, that is, in youth also it can happen. *Sarvamapyathavā bhogaṁ manyamāno virūpakam*, or those persons who are fed up with enjoyment of worldly enjoyment, who are fed up, who hate worldly enjoyments. Although they are likely to, fit to enjoy this [world], but they hate it, *sarvamapyathavā bhogaṁ, sarva bhogam manyamāno virūpakam*, they consider this *tamaśa* (drama) a waste of time, *utkrama*, there is the possibility for him also to get extracted from this life and united in God consciousness. There is no fear that when he experiences death of that body, that young body, a young body also, he leaves that body and can be sentenced to God consciousness. And there is no fear of the remaining portion of his *bhoga* will remain untouched. The remaining portion of his *bhoga* will exhaust in the ether.

JOHN: His enjoyment (*bhoga*), what he has left? Is that *karma*, you mean?

SWAMIJI: *Karma*, he'll have no *karma* left. Because of this experiencing that, "This *bhoga* is *bakwas* (nonsense), I hate this, it is useless," for him this is the way to fly at once to God consciousness. These two *śloka*s are meant for him.

JOHN: So the master has to do something to extract that person?

SWAMIJI: Huh?

JOHN: Master has to do something for that person?

SWAMIJI: Yes, it is called *utkrānti dīkṣā*. *Utkrānti dīkṣā* [is to] take that soul away from that body with meditation, with contemplation. He contemplates on that body. Who?

DENISE: The master.

SWAMIJI: The master, and he extracts the ego, extracts the soul from that body and there is [only] a dead body left and he goes, he is sentenced to God consciousness. *Bas*. So he lives in peace.

I cannot read it, this third one.
JOHN: *Tāmāśrityor…*
SWAMIJI: Ah, yes. It is the *śloka*s of the *Spanda Śāstra*.

Wisdom Verses 4 (8:19)

तामाश्रित्योर्ध्वमार्गेण चन्द्रसूर्यावुभावपि ।
सौषुम्नेऽध्वन्यस्तमितो हित्वा ब्रह्माण्डगोचरम् ॥४५॥
तदा तस्मिन्महाव्योम्नि प्रलीनशशिभास्करे ।
सौषुप्तपदवन्मूढः प्रबुद्धः स्यादनावृतः ॥४६॥
(निलकं)

tāmāśrityordhvamārgeṇa candrasūryāvubhāvapi /
sauṣumne'dhvanyastamito hitvā brahmāṇḍagocaram //45//
tadā tasminmahāvyomni pralīnaśaśibhāskare /
sauṣuptapadavanmūḍhaḥ prabuddhaḥ syādanāvṛtaḥ //46//

These are two *śloka*s to be kept together (Swamiji repeats the verses).

Tāmāśrityordhva mārgeṇa, that supreme state of God consciousness you should long and desire to possess (the *sādhaka*, the aspirant, should long and desire to possess that state), *ūrdhva mārgeṇa*, but you have to long and possess by the *ūrdhva mārga* (*ūrdhva mārga* means, by the pathway of the upper path).

There is an internal path, external path, and upper path. The internal path is that of the in-going breath, the external path is that of the out-coming breath, and the upper path is the point, the central point of these two breaths, which is likely to be found, experienced between the two eyebrows or in the throat pit or at the center of the heart. Those are three points where there is hope of…this is the entering point, the entering point for the upper path. So you have to wait there, you have to knock [on] it. You have to knock [on] it only just in a flash, a flash of knocking. Go on breathing inside, then you breathe out, and when you breathe in, just give a little push of knocking there, the knocking of just alertness. Just be alert there at the automatic point of the junction.

JOHN: At the point of breathing out, before you start to breathe in, that...

SWAMIJI: At that point.

JOHN: And also when you breathe in, before you breathe out, the same?

SWAMIJI: Yes, the same.

JOHN: Both places.

SWAMIJI: Both places. It is an internal point and external point, both.

JOHN: So that's what you mean by "knocking"?

SWAMIJI: That is knocking.

JOHN: And your attention should be either here, between the eyebrows, or in the throat pit or...

SWAMIJI: Or in the heart, yes.

JOHN: But you don't recommend the heart.

SWAMIJI: I recommend only between the two eyebrows because my master also recommended that, and I experienced it successful.

Candra sūryāu ubhāvapi, then that yogi who is doing this practice in continuity,...*

Just knocking and come down, knocking and come down, knock and come down. There is no room to wait. Waiting there is prohibited. You have to go knock and come down, go knock and come down. Just do knocking with love and devotion and come down. Each time, each time you go, just knock and come down.

JOHN: So we don't believe in suspending the breath, holding the breath at that point.

SWAMIJI: No, you have not to hold it, that is the wrong way. Nothing will come out by that. You have to go there, knock, and come down. This is the trick, which you have to...

*...*candra sūryāu ubhāvapi*, the time will come [when] *candra sūryāu ubhāvapi*, both breaths, inhale and exhale, both breaths will automatically...they will be balled, they will be balled in sometime, sometime they will be balled together. You know "balling"? They will be balled together and they will sink in the central vein...

JOHN: "Balled together" means?

SWAMIJI:...by that opening. There will be an opening. By knocking, the door will be opened. Again knock, again knock, knock, knock,

knock, knock, and the door will be opened. I don't know when. It may take one month, it may take two years, it may take a hundred years, it may take three lives, it may take numberless lives, but go on knocking! You have not to wait, go on doing it. Have this faith that it will be opened, and it will be opened.

JOHN: So God opens the door. You only have to knock, He has to open.

SWAMIJI: No, it will be opened automatically. It is automatic.

JOHN: But "automatic" means that it would come automatically, you knock and then it opens, but you say it may take one life, it may take one day, it may take one week…

SWAMIJI: It depends upon your devotion, how you knock it. At the time of knocking, you should crave, you should implore, you should die [for it], you should love it.

JOHN: "Please, open the door."

SWAMIJI: No, you have not to cry. Crying will make it worse. You should not call. Just long, just desire.

SHANNA: Inside.

SWAMIJI: Inside, yes. *Sauṣumne'dhvan yasta mitaḥ hitvā brahmāṇḍa gocaram*, then they will get absorbed in the central vein, both breaths, *tadā tasmin mahā vyomni pralīna śaśi bhaskare*, and in that great ether where breathing in and breathing out have altogether vanished, there also if you are not alert, if you have not maintained awareness, alertness, you will become *mūḍhaḥ* (*mūḍhaḥ* means, just paralyzed), you will become paralyzed. And that person who is maintaining alertness altogether, [he can experience that state in the daily routine of life also].[18] Because it has so much taste, you will sink in that, you will sink in that taste, you will sink in that taste and lose consciousness, you will lose consciousness, you will lose that joy. But as soon as you lose that joy, finished, your whole thing is no use.

DENISE: Well, what do you maintain alertness on when it's all balled together, in-going and out-going breaths all balled together? Where do you maintain that alertness?

SWAMIJI: You have to watch each and every movement of that.

---

18. Swamiji did not complete the translation here. The inserted text was taken from Swamiji's original translation of this verse from the *Spanda Kārikā* (1.25).

DENISE: Just watch what it's doing.

SWAMIJI: You have not to be taken by that joy, ecstasy…

DENISE: Not to get sunk in it.

SWAMIJI:…sunk in that ecstasy.

DENISE: Just be aware of its movement, internal movement.

SWAMIJI: Internal movement. But internal ecstasy you should also, you should not…

JOHN: Not to lose your awareness?

SWAMIJI: By that ecstasy, you should not lose your awareness.

DENISE: So do you ignore the ecstasy? You ignore it? You try to ignore it?

SWAMIJI: You have to try to ignore it [and think], "I have to do my duty, let it come, let it come this ecstasy all-around, let me sink in that ecstasy, I don't care, I want my duty to be done," then everything is hopeful. *Prabuddhaḥ syāt anāvṛtaḥ*, *prabuddha*, you are alert, fully alert, but that ecstasy will push you away from that.

DENISE: It will intoxicate you.

SWAMIJI: You will be intoxicated and you will think that you have gained everything, but that you should not do, it will be a blunder, a great mistake.

JOHN: So *mūḍhaḥ* means that you go to sleep then, you fall asleep, you just go to that deep sleep?

SWAMIJI: No, you get…

DENISE: Drowsy?

SWAMIJI:…drowsy in that state. You'll not be capable of holding that ecstasy anymore if alertness is gone.

JOHN: If you become drowsy, then what happens? *Mūḍhaḥ* means?

SWAMIJI: *Mūḍhaḥ* means, you become drowsy in that happiness.

JOHN: And then you go to sleep? You said before that you always leave the state of *samādhi* and go into sleep.

SWAMIJI: Yes, you come down. So, it's terrible…that highest stage is also…there is a diversion. Because this is a great achievement. A great achievement is not easily achieved. You will go astray with that ecstasy.

DENISE: For sure, everybody goes astray or some people remain alert?

SWAMIJI: Some remain alert who are handled by the master very carefully, and whom masters love very much. *Bas*, we will do only this much.

JOHN: So this is not the *Tantrāloka* here, this verse.
SWAMIJI: This is *Spanda*.
JOHN: *Spanda Kārikās*?
SWAMIJI: Of Vasugupta. *Spanda Nirṇaya*, you have that?[19]
JOHN: Yes, we have all those done by you. So what you have done, you have gathered together all important *śloka*s from different...
SWAMIJI: Yes, I have put in that.
JOHN:...places.
SWAMIJI: It is for your daily recitation. Maybe sometime you will experience these stages. I did this there [in my ashram], did [the compilation of] these *śloka*s with this intention that I would tell you.
DENISE: Really? That's so great.
SWAMIJI: I had in my mind to write to you in details, but I had not this thought that God would make it true.
JOHN: That we would be here together?
SWAMIJI: Yes.
DENISE: How long ago did you do this, compile this?
SWAMIJI: I think it took one year.
JOHN: Do you have verse numbers and information like that? Is that existing somewhere?
SWAMIJI: This is not that [kind of] research. You should not do that. Give it numbers, regular numbers. Make it as another independent book for your recitation. It will be helpful to you in *sādhana* (practice).
JOHN: Yes, I agree with that.

Wisdom Verses 4 (23:17)

यामवस्थां समालम्ब्य यदयं मम वक्ष्यति ।
तदवश्यं करिष्येऽहमिति संकल्प्य तिष्ठति ॥४७॥

yāmavasthāṁ samālambya yadayaṁ mama vakṣyati /
tadavaśyaṁ kariṣye'hamiti saṁkalpya tiṣṭhati //47//

19. Abhinavagupta's principal disciple, Kṣemarāja, wrote a commentary on the *Spanda Karikā* called the *Spanda Nirṇaya*.

Yāmavasthāṁ samālambya, when a yogi takes hold, catches hold of that *avastha* (state), that state of *turya*, the beginning of *turya*, when a yogi takes hold of that state which is felt at the beginning of *turya*, when he is likely to go in *samādhi*, he has not yet gone in *samādhi*, before going [into] that he takes an oath in his own self according to the directions of his master: "*yadayaṁ mama vakṣyati*, you go ahead according to that which you are taught from within, you have not to listen to my directions afterwards." When you are about to enter in *samādhi*, then you have to do according to the directions which come [from] above in *samādhi*. You have to go ahead according to the directions of *samādhi*, not according to the directions of *śāstra*s or according to the directions of the master. The master's job is over there when he is likely…when he is going inside. So, "*tad avaśyaṁ kariṣye'ham*, that I will do definitely what is informed [to] me [from] within at that time of going in. *Tad avaśyaṁ kariṣye'ham*, I will do that definitely." *Iti saṁkalpya tiṣṭhati*, so he has to remain there with this oath that, "Whatever is felt within me, whatever order is felt within me from myself, that I have to obey." It is the direction which he gets from his master. Up to that point, he has to tread according to the directions of the master. Afterwards, the master's job is over.

Then, what happens next? That he says in this [next *śloka*]. This is the *śloka* of the *Bhagavad Gītā*:

Wisdom Verses 4 (27:02)

Yogasya Mahatvam (Bhagavad Gītā)
The Essence of Yoga

यत्रोपरमते चित्तं निरुद्धं योगसेवनात् ।
यत्र चैवात्मनात्मानं पश्यन्नात्मनि तुष्यति ॥४८॥
सुखमात्यन्तिकं यत्तद्बुद्धिग्राह्यमतीन्द्रियम् ।
वेत्ति यत्र न चैवायं स्थितश्चलति तत्त्वतः ॥४९॥
यं लब्ध्वा चापरं लाभं मन्यते नाधिकं ततः ।

यस्मिन् स्थितो न दुःखेन गुरुणापि विचाल्यते ॥५०॥
तं विद्याद्दुःखसंयोगवियोगं योगसंज्ञितम् ।
स निश्चयेन योक्तव्यो योगोऽनिर्वण्णचेतसा ॥५१॥

yatroparamate cittaṁ niruddhaṁ yogasevanāt /
yatra caivātmanātmānaṁ paśyannātmani tuṣyati //48//
sukhamātyantikaṁ yattadbuddhigrāhyamatīndriyam /
vetti yatra na caivāyaṁ sthitaścalati tattvataḥ //49//
yaṁ labdhvā cāparaṁ lābhaṁ manyate nādhikaṁ tataḥ /
yasmin sthito na duḥkhena guruṇāpi vicālyate //50//
taṁ vidyādduḥkhasaṁyogaviyogaṁ yogasaṁjñitam /
sa niścayena yoktavyo yogo'nirviṇṇacetasā //51//

I'll show you how to note it down. Give me a pencil. Thank you. *Kulakam* means, it has got connection with all these.

JOHN: It's all one connection, one connected meaning.

SWAMIJI: Yes. Like this. Now I will explain the meaning of this.

Yatroparamate cittaṁ, there, when he takes this vow according to the directions of his master, that, "I have to do accordingly what I will feel that has been ordered within," after taking this vow perfectly, the time comes he has to *uparamate cittaṁ*, *niruddhaṁ cittaṁ*, his mind, the *sādhaka*'s mind, the mind of the *sādhaka* becomes, takes the position of, *niruddha avasthā*.

There are so many stages of mind, one's mind. One is *kṣipta*, the first is *kṣipta*, the second is *vikṣipta*, the third is *ekāgra*, the fourth is *niruddha*. *Kṣipta* means, e.g., when you think, "This is a tape recorder" or "This is a pencil," without any meaning what for you are thinking.

DENISE: The mind just moves from one thing to the next?

SWAMIJI: Yes, without any purpose. "This is a book." What to you? "This is a pen." So you go on thinking like this. It is *kṣipta* (*kṣipta* means, scattered, scattered mind). This is the position of a scattered mind, it has nothing to do with yoga. Yoga is absolutely away from this state of mind. This is the first state, ordinary state of the life of a human being. What is this called? This is called *kṣipta*, the *kṣipta* state. The second state is *vikṣipta*. *Vikṣipta* is now when you want to control this [mind but] it goes away, it goes away. You want to keep your mind one-pointed [but] it goes away, it goes away at once. You want to keep it one-pointed, for instance, [between] the eyebrows, you put your consciousness and mind in [between the two] eyebrows, [but] it goes away to another object. Then it goes away to another object and you collect awareness after sometime, you don't collect awareness at that very moment.

JOHN: Because you don't realize that your mind went away.

SWAMIJI:...went away, you are unaware, at that time you are unaware. And afterwards you think, "Oh, I was meditating. What have I done? I am thinking of an *almira* (wardrobe) now." That is the position of the mind [which] is called *vikṣipta*. Then comes the third state of the mind when you are bent upon putting [awareness] on one point with concentration. That is called *ekāgra*, one-pointed. When you keep it one-pointed, it tries to go away, it tries to go away; every now and then it tries to go away to some other object, to some other object. You have to be attentive in such a way that you don't let it go to that object. Before [the mind] goes to [that] object, you drive [it] back to [its] own point. This is the state of mind which is called *ekāgra*. Then you have to go like this. This also has nothing to do with yoga. *Samādhi* is not possible in this way also. And afterwards, the state of the mind comes in such a way that it becomes *niruddha*, it does not go away at all. [Even] if you drive it away, it won't go, it will go to one point. That is *nirudhha avasthā*, that is, when this mind has taken the position of *niruddha avasthā*. *Niruddha avasthā* is one-pointedness, automatic, when you have not to drive [the mind] again back and back to return to [its] point. Returning ends at the ending stage of *ekāgra*. When *ekāgra* is finished, then you have not to drive it [to one-pointedness] again and again. That process is over. You have to watch then, how it is absorbed in one-pointedness. That is called *niruddha avasthā*. And this *niruddha avasthā* comes, or *yoga sevanāt*, by the continuity of practice, meditation. Then you have not to drive it [to one-pointedness] again and again.

DENISE: It's automatic.

SWAMIJI: Automatic. *Niruddhaṁ cittaṁ*, *yogasevanāt*, by the practice of yoga, *niruddhaṁ cittaṁ*, when your mind becomes *niruddha*, takes the position of its being one-pointed for good,...*

If you leave it open, leave this mind free, it won't go away. You have not to be watchful afterwards. Watchfulness ends at the ending point of *ekāgra*. You have not to be watchful after it takes the position of *niruddha avasthā*. At that time, you will rest, you have not to be watchful.

*...*niruddhaṁ yogasevanāt*, by the practice of yoga, the continuity of yoga, this mind, when it takes the position of *niruddha avasthā*, *yatra uparamate*, where this mind automatically ceases to function (it does not function in the way it was [usually] going to do this function, the function of going here and there), *yatra caivātmanātmānaṁ paśyann-ātmani tuṣyati*, and where *ātmanā ātamānaṁ paśyan*, he realizes the nature of his own Self consciousness, and *ātmani tuṣyati*, and he is satisfied with enjoying the bliss of Self consciousness, at that time, *sukhamātyantikaṁ yattat*, he experiences the *sukha*–this is the second *śloka*–at that time he experiences the *sukha* (*sukha* means, joy)–what kind of joy?–*ātyantikaṁ*, where there is no parallel, there is no parallel joy to it. That joy he experiences at that moment when he realizes the nature of his own Self–at that moment. It is tremendous joy he experiences. And that joy is not seen by the eyes, it is not felt by your organs. *Buddhi grāhyam*, it is felt by your intellect only, internal intellect, super-intellect. Patāñjalī describes this intellect as *ṛtaṁ bharā*, it is filled with...*ṛtaṁ* means, truth.[20] It is truth, true joy, it is not adjusted joy. Adjusted joy takes position in the contact of two [things], and this is not adjusted joy, it is automatic joy. So he feels automatic joy. *Atīndriyam*, it is beyond the conduct of the organs. The organs are not conducting this joy. Where this joy is felt, *na caivāyaṁ sthitaścalati tattvataḥ*, and when he is absolutely established in that joy, *na calati tattvataḥ*, then he does not move from that joy at all.

There is another point to be watched and marked there at that time: *Yaṁ labdhvā*, when this joy is achieved, this automatic joy, *aparaṁ lābhaṁ manyate nādhikaṁ*, then he feels there is not any other joy like this in all of the one hundred and eighteen worlds. This is the only joy which one has to possess and own.

JOHN: Unparalleled.

SWAMIJI: Unparalleled, yes. You can't imagine the fullness of that joy. *Nādhikaṁ tataḥ*, he does not feel any other joy like this. *Yasmin sthito*, when he is established once in that joy, *na duḥkhena guruṇāpi vicālyate*, even if heaps of tortures come in front of him, heaps of pains

---

20. *Yoga Sūtras* 1.48.

come in his experience, *na vicālyate*, he is not moved by those. He is not at all moved by those pains and sorrows and sadnesses of the world. This sadness of the world, if it comes to him, it appears as if it is in that joyous position. [Sadness] is just like [the sensation of] scratching a little bit, *bas*, that also is joyful.

DENISE: Like what?

SWAMIJI: Just scratching like this, *bas*, no more. It is fun for him afterwards. It becomes fun, it is not saddening.

JOHN: Anything in this world.

SWAMIJI: Any torture, any pain, he feels just additional joy.

DENISE: It's sugar-coated pain.

SWAMIJI: It's sugar-coated, yes (laughs).

DENISE: Sugar-coated pain and torture.

Wisdom Verses 4 (41:30) end
Wisdom Verses 5 (00:12) start

SWAMIJI: The last *śloka* is in this connection: *Taṁ vidyāt duḥkha saṁyoga viyogaṁ yoga saṁjñitam*, you should understand, one should understand, the aspirant should understand, that this joy which he is feeling within, and where in which joy all pains and sorrows of the world, if they come, if they are experienced, they enhance the beauty of that joy, they do not disturb that joy at all to him, that joy you should consider (*vidyāt*, you should think and you should know) *duḥkha saṁyoga viyogaṁ*, it is the absence of all pain. No pain has the guts to stand there (*taṁ vidyāt duḥkha saṁyoga viyogaṁ*). And it is *yoga saṁjñitam*, it is called yoga, actually it is yoga, it is the state of yoga. *Sa niścayena yoktavyo yogo nirviṇṇacetasā*, and that yoga should be contemplated and achieved by a *sādhaka* with *nirviṇṇa-cetasā*. It can be explained as *anirviṇṇa cetasā* and *nirviṇṇa cetasā*, both ways. *Nirviṇṇa cetasā* means, when he becomes totally absent from worldly pleasures. Not absent, actually, not absent, he does not mean to leave them aside. He wants to find out the joy in those worldly pleasures also, because he feels that joy is everywhere, joy is in worldly pleasures also–that joy, that super joy.

DEVOTEE: So nothing is to be excluded.

SWAMIJI: Yes.

DENISE: He is not afraid of anything.

SWAMIJI: Everything is included there. So, you should try to experience that joy with not being bored to have it. When you taste the sweetest dish in the world, go on tasting the sweetest dishes, sweetest dishes, you will be bored by that. In time, you will be bored (laughs), you will want to have some *chutney* afterwards.

DENISE: Something sour.

SWAMIJI: Something sour. But that does not take place in this experience of this joy. This is not boring joy. You want to have it again and again the same way.

DENISE: Nourishing.

SWAMIJI: Nourishing, it is nourishing.

JOHN: You crave after it, is it? I mean, you never get enough.

DENISE: But you never lose it also, right?

SWAMIJI: No, you want to have it again and again.

JOHN: That's what I mean: you never get enough.

SWAMIJI: No (affirmative).

Wisdom Verses 5 (3:52)

प्रशान्तमनसं ह्येनं योगिनं सुखमुत्तमम् ।
उपैति शान्तरजसं ब्रह्मभूतमकल्मषम् ॥५२॥

praśāntamanasaṁ hyenaṁ yoginaṁ sukhamuttamam /
upaiti śāntarajasaṁ brahmabhūtamakalmaṣam //52//

Praśānta manasaṁ, that yogi whose mind is *praśānta*, whose mind is appeased from all sides (there is no need to worry about his position of mind, his mind is appeased, it has come to this perfect state of being appeased), *yoginaṁ*, for that kind of yogi, *sukham uttamam upaiti*, *praśānta manasaṁ hyenaṁ yoginaṁ*, the yogi becomes an object there. The yogi has not to find out the reality of God, the reality of the nature of God–the yogi has not to find it. The nature of God has to find this yogi. That is what he says: *praśānta manasaṁ hyenaṁ*, it is objective, he has to become an object, the yogi has to become the object for this joy. Joy has to go to him, joy will find the yogi, joy wants to find out that yogi.

DENISE: Which yogi?

SWAMIJI: Who has an appeased mind. So joy is after finding out, in search of that yogi. The yogi has not to search [for] joy. That is Abhinavagupta's interpretation of that *Bhagavad Gītā* verse.

JOHN: So what that means is that the yogi…

SWAMIJI: The yogi has to remain passive, he is not active. He is not active, joy is active.

JOHN: So this is automatic. This is that point in the sipping down [of breath] where, from then on, God carries you, you don't do anything, there is nothing to do from your side.

SWAMIJI: You have nothing to do. Don't worry about God. God has to worry about you at that moment. When your mind is appeased, then don't worry about anything. God will find you because God is in search of you. God will be subjective and you will remain the object, passive. Action is to be taken by God. You have not to take any action, you remain as you are, don't worry about anything, it is His headache to find you. That is what He says in this *śloka*.

Praśānta manasaṁ hyenaṁ yoginaṁ sukham uttamam upaiti śānta rajasaṁ, this is *śānta rajasaṁ*, where all the activity of the world is appeased. *Brahma bhūtam*, he is absolutely one with God, he has become one with God. Why should he worry about God? God has to search [for] him. *Akalmaṣam*, he is without any *kalmaṣa* (*akalmaṣa* means, there is no dirt, without dirt), he is absolutely clean. He has a clean mind, he has no dirt in his nature…

DENISE: You mean, no *mala*s?

SWAMIJI: No *mala*s.[21] And God is bent upon finding him. He has

---

21. "The three impurities (*mala*s) are gross (*sthūla*), subtle (*sūkṣma*), and subtlest (*para*). The gross impurity is called *kārmamala.* It is connected with actions. It is that impurity which inserts impressions such as those which are expressed in the statements, "I am happy," "I am not well," "I have pain," "I am a great man," "I am really lucky," etcetera, in the consciousness of the individual being. The next impurity is called *māyīyamala*. This impurity creates differentiation in one's own consciousness. It is the impurity of ignorance (*avidyā*), the subtle impurity. The thoughts, "This house is mine," "That house is not mine," "This man is my friend," "That man is my enemy," "She is my wife," "She is not my wife," are all created by *māyīyamala*. *Māyīyamala* creates duality. The third impurity is called *āṇavamala*. It is the subtlest impurity. *Āṇavamala* is the particular internal impurity of the

to remain lying on a sofa.

DENISE: Just waiting.

SWAMIJI: Yes (laughs). Why should he wait?

DENISE: Not even waiting.

SWAMIJI: It is His headache to see him.

DENISE: He is fine already, he is appeased.

SWAMIJI: Yes.

Wisdom Verses 5 (7:59)

युञ्जन्नेवं सदात्मानं योगी नियतमानसः ।
सुखेन ब्रह्मसंयोगमत्यन्तमधिगच्छति ॥५३॥
(कुलकं)

yuñjannevaṁ sadātmānaṁ yogī niyatamānasaḥ /
sukhena brahmasaṁyogamatyantamadhigacchati //53//

Yuñjannevaṁ sadāt mānaṁ, this way you should contemplate always, the yogi should contemplate this way, *niyata mānasaḥ*, and keeping his mind absolutely under control, full control. Full control means that *niruddha avasthā*, when [the mind] keeps quiet, it does

---

individual. Although he reaches the nearest state of the consciousness of Śiva, he has no ability to catch hold of that state. That inability is the creation of *āṇavamala*. For example, if you are conscious of your own nature and then that consciousness fades away, and fades away quickly, this fading is caused by *āṇavamala*. *Āṇavamala* is *apūrṇatā*, non-fullness. It is the feeling of being incomplete. Due to this impurity, you feel incomplete in every way. Though you feel incomplete, knowing that there is some lack in you, yet you do not know what this lack really is. You want to hold everything, and yet no matter what you hold, you do not fill your sense of lacking, your gap. You cannot fill this lacking unless the master points it out to you and then carries you to that point. Of these three impurities, *āṇavamala* and *māyīyamala* are not in action, they are only in perception, in experience. It is *kārmamala* which is in action." *Kashmir Shaivism–The Secret Supreme*, 7.47-49.

not move. If you are away also, if you are not attending your mind, the mind has no guts to move, it won't move, it is appeased. This way the yogi should act: *sukhena*, he has not to put effort to realize this position of God then. *Sukhena* (playfully), *brahma-saṁyogam atyantam*, he becomes one with supreme God consciousness playfully. Without doing any effort, he attains the state of God consciousness for all times.

And for this, the one who is going to practice this way, for him there is the liability of obstacles. Obstacles will take place for him–in the beginning, not in the end when his mind takes the position of *niruddha avasthā*. Obstacles are functioning only up to the end of *ekāgra*, not at the time when his mind takes the state of *niruddha avasthā*, then there are no obstacles. Till then, there are obstacles.

Wisdom Verses 5 (10:39)

विघ्नायुतसहस्रं तु परोत्साहसमन्वितम् ।
प्रहरत्यनिशं जन्तोः सद्वस्त्वभिमुखस्य च ।
विशेषतो भवाम्बोधिसमुत्तरणकारिणः ॥५४॥

vighnāyutasahasraṁ tu parotsāhasamanvitam /
praharatyaniśaṁ jantoḥ sadvastvabhimukhasya ca /
viśeṣato bhavāmbodhisamuttaraṇakāriṇaḥ //54//

This one *śloka* and a half *śloka* is from that…which *śāstra*?

JOHN: *Vivṛti Vimarśinī.*

SWAMIJI: *Vivṛti Vimarśinī*, yes, of Abhinavagupta. *Vighna ayuta sahasraṁ tu*, obstacles–not one, not two, not three, not four–*ayuta sahasraṁ* (*ayuta* means, ten *lakhs*[22], *sahasraṁ tu*, into one thousand), one thousand and ten *lakh*s [of] these obstacles…

JOHN: Lots of obstacles.

SWAMIJI:…rise at once! *Parotsāha samanvitam*, with great strength, with great vigor they rise to attack that person. *Vighna ayuta*

22. One *lakh* is 100,000.

sahasraṁ tu parotsāha samanvitam, with great vigor they rise, *praharati*, and they attack *jantoḥ*, that individual, *sadva stvabhimukhasya*, who wants to do good things, who wants to act piously. For him, these obstacles arise. How many obstacles?

JOHN: *Lakh*s.

SWAMIJI: Ten *lakh*s into one thousand (1000 million).

JOHN: Lots.

SWAMIJI: (laughs) *Viśeṣato*, and more than that number. These obstacles arise for him, *bhavāmbodhi samuttaraṇa-kāriṇaḥ*, who wants to get liberated and get merged in God consciousness. For him, there is some bigger force of obstacles.

DENISE: Worse.

SWAMIJI: Worst.

JOHN: So this is from where?

SWAMIJI: This is from *Tantra*.

JOHN: *Tantrāloka*?

SWAMIJI: Yes, it is from the *Tantra*.[23]

Wisdom Verses 5 (13:03)

रामः किमुच्यते देव योऽत्रस्थः स च कः प्रभो ।
तस्याभ्यासः कथं नाम ब्रूहि मे परमेश्वर ॥५५॥

rāmaḥ kimucyate deva yo'trasthaḥ sa ca kaḥ prabho /
tasyābhyāsaḥ kathaṁ nāma brūhi me parameśvara //55//

Iti praśnagranthaḥ, praśnagranthaḥ means it is a question raised by Pārvatī to Lord Śiva: *Rāmaḥ kimucyate deva*, O Deva, O Lord, what is the meaning of "Rāma"? I want to get an exposition of Rāma, what is Rāma, what is meant by this word "Rāma," who is Rāma.[24] And the one who is

23. As Swamiji said previously, this verse is from Abhinavagupta's *Pratyabhijñā Vivṛti Vimarśinī*.

24. "Rāma is *paramātmā*, the supreme God consciousness." *Tantrāloka* 1.85 (LJA archive).

established in the state of Rāma, who is that person? Who must be that person? *Yo'trasthaḥ*, that person who is established in Rāma, *sa ca kaḥ prabho*, who is that person? Is he a yogi? Is he ancient? Who is he?

This is the question put by Pārvatī to Śiva.

Tasyābhyāsaḥ kathaṁ nāma, how can the meditation upon Rāma be conducted? *Brūhi me parameśvara*, please, explain this to Me. I am fond of meditating upon this Rāma, who is Rāma.

Iti praśnagranthaḥ, this *śloka* is lying in *praśna*, in enquiry. It is an enquiry made by Pārvatī. She wants to know who is Rāma, and who is established in Rāma, and how can Rāma be contemplated upon. *Atra uttara granthaḥ*, now this is *uttara granthaḥ*, this is the…

VIRESH: Answer?

SWAMIJI:…answer, yes. *Uttara* means, answer, yes. They also understand a little bit. *Atra uttara granthaḥ*, now He explains what is "Rāma":

Wisdom Verses 5 (16:00)

गतिः स्थानं स्वप्नजाग्रदुन्मेषणनिमेषणे ।
धावनं प्लवनं चैव आयासः शक्तिवेदनम् ॥५६॥
बुद्धिभेदास्तथा भावाः संज्ञाः कर्माण्यनेकशः ।
एतच्चतुर्दशविधं रामं तु परिकीर्तितम् ॥५७॥
ऊर्ध्वं त्यक्त्वाधो विशेत् स रामस मध्यदेशगः ॥
(युगलकं)

gatiḥ sthānaṁ svapnajāgradunmeṣaṇanimeṣaṇe /
dhāvaṇaṁ plavanaṁ caiva āyāsaḥ śaktivedanam //56//
buddhibhedāstathā bhāvāḥ saṁjñāḥ karmāṇyanekaśaḥ /
etaccaturdaśavidhaṁ rāmaṁ tu parikīrtitam //57//

Rāma is fourteenfold actually. This is the answer that came from the divine lips of Her daddy (laughs).

JOHN: *Pati*.

SWAMIJI: *Pati*, yes. *Gatiḥ* (walking), just walk and you'll find the state of Rāma. *Sthānaṁ*, just sit, you'll find the state of Rāma. *Gatiḥ* means, walking, in walking. *Sthānaṁ* means, in sitting. *Svapna* (in dreaming), *jāgrat* (in wakefulness), *unmesaṇa* (in the twinkling of your eyes open, keeping your eyelids open), *nimeṣaṇa* (keeping your eyelids closed), there is Rāma. *Dhāvaṇaṁ*, running, fast running, there is Rāma. *Plavanaṁ*, jumping, there is Rāma (*plavanaṁ caiva*). *Āyāsaḥ*, ignorance, forgetfulness, that is Rāma–*āyāsaḥ*. *Śakti vedanam*, deriving strength from within for killing some enemy, that strength, with force you want to kill him, that is Rāma. That is *śakti vedanam*. *Buddhi bhedā*, *buddhi bedhā* means the eightfold sections of *buddhi*s (intellect): *dharma* (proper action), *jñāna* (knowledge), *vairagya* (detachment), *aiśvarya* (power); *adharma* (improper action), *ajñāna* (ignorance), *avairāgya* (attachment), *anaiśvarya* (weakness). *Dharma* means to adopt your duty. *Adharma* means the negation of your duty. How many?

DENISE: Two.

SWAMIJI: Two. *Dharma*, *adharma*, *jñāna* (knowledge), *ajñāna*...

JOHN: Ignorance.

SWAMIJI: Ignorance. *Dharma*, *adharma*, *jñāna*, *ajñāna*, and *vairagya*. *Vairagya* means detachment. *Aiśvarya* means attachment. *Dharma*, *ajñāna*, *vairagya*, *aiśvarya*, *anaiśvarya*. *Dharma*, *jñāna*, *vairagya* and *aiśvarya*. *Adharma*, *ajñāna*, *avairagya*, and *anaiśvarya*.

JOHN: So what is...? *Vairagya* means?

SWAMIJI: Not Bhairava, it is...

JOHN: *Vairagya*, *vairagya*.

SWAMIJI: *Vairagya* means detachment.

JOHN: And *avairagya* means?

SWAMIJI: Attachment.

JOHN: And then *aiśvarya* means?

SWAMIJI: *Dharma* means duty. *Adharma*...*jñāna* means knowledge. First...

JOHN: Yes, first is the positive part.

SWAMIJI: Positive part. *Dharma*, *jñāna*, *vairagya*. *Vairagya* means detachment. *Aiśvarya* means the glory of Lord Śiva. This is one section of four. Another four is the opposite section. *Adharma*, *adharma* means...it is vice?

JOHN: Vice? No, uh...

SWAMIJI: Acting in vice. Virtue and vice. It is opposite to virtue. That is *adharma*.

JOHN: Forsaking your duty. If you have something dutiful, you can forsake that.

SWAMIJI: Forsake that, ignore that. That is *adharma*. *Ajñāna* means ignorance. *Adharma*, *ajñāna*, *avairagya* (attachment), *anaiśvarya* (not *aiśvarya*).

JOHN: What is that?

SWAMIJI: *Anaiśvarya*, absence of being glorious, when you are, *bas*, pitiable, when you remain in a pitiable condition as Samvit Prakash was there [in Delhi]. I felt him in a pitiable...

DENISE: Degraded.

SWAMIJI: Degraded, yes. (indaudible) Everywhere! Rāma is all-pervading, in a good way or in a bad way also.

JOHN: So He is in everything. In everything and in the negation of everything also.

SWAMIJI: *Gatiḥ sthānaṁ svapna jāgrat unmesaṇa nimeṣaṇe buddhibedha*, these are *buddhibedha*. *Buddhibedha* means, the sections of *buddhi*s,...

JOHN: Yes, intellect.

SWAMIJI:...sections of understanding. These are how many? Eight: *dharma*, *jñāna*, *vairagya*, *aiśvarya*–four; and the second opposite four: *adharma*, *ajñāna*, *avairagya*, *anaiśvarya*–these four. *Tathā bhāvāḥ*, and whatever objective world you see before you, that is Rāma, that is *buddhi bhāvāḥ*. *Saṁjñāḥ karmaṇya*; *saṁjñāḥ* means, names, e.g., Denise, Viresh, Shanna, Inderji, Lakṣmanjoo, John, Jonathan, George, tiles, tables, pens, pencils, tape recorders, video tapes. All these names and formations of these things [are Rāma]. And *karmaṇya*, actions, various actions in this world, which are felt in movement, in the functioning of this world, [are Rāma]. *Etat caturdaśa vidhaṁ*, this fourteenfold everything, *rāmaṁ tu parikīrtitam*, is the position, the state of, Rāma. You must find out the state of Rāma in all this. So, in each and every activity, positive or negative, in all activities you will find the state of Rāma.

When you once find the state of Rāma, what happens to you? He says in the next verses:

Wisdom Verses 5 (23:37)

ऊर्ध्वं त्त्वाधो विशेत् स रामस्थो मध्यदेशगः ॥५८॥

ūrdhvaṁ tyaktvādho viśet sa rāmastho madhyadeśagaḥ //58//

Bas, only a half *śloka* (verse repeated).

Ūrdhvaṁ tyaktvā, after [having] discarded the activity of the top, after [having] discarded the activity of the bottom, *viśet*, just enter in the center, you'll be established in Rāma. And that is the establishment held in the central vein (*madhya nāḍī*). This you have to find. If you want to find out in the yogic way, then you can find out this way.[25] Who? Whom you will find?

JOHN: Rāma.

SWAMIJI: Rāma. Otherwise, if you don't want to find Rāma in the yogic way, then find Him in the universal way. He is everywhere. The universal way is also fine, finer than the yogic way, and the yogic way is also finer than the universal way. They are both delicious.

JOHN: So the yogic way is to…

SWAMIJI: The best.

JOHN:…is to take one action, leave that action, and go to the center?

SWAMIJI: Yes. And the universal way is to be in the universe and contact the position of Rāma everywhere.

DENISE: What does it mean to take one action, leave that action, and go to the center?

SWAMIJI: Huh?

DENISE: What do you mean? Take one action…

SWAMIJI: Not action.

DENISE: What were you just saying, John?

JOHN: The yogic way of finding Rāma.

---

25. "Up and down in *āṇavopāya* is breath, the two breaths. In *śāktopāya* it is *pramāṇa* and *prameya*. And in *śāmbhavopya* it is *prakāśa* and *vimarśa*." *Tantrāloka* 1.85 (LJA archive).

SWAMIJI: That is, the yogic way of finding Rāma is just to leave the top away, leave the bottom away, enter in the center. That is the yogic way.

DENISE: Like between two breaths?

SWAMIJI: Between two breaths, between two steps, between two talks, between two movements. Chew your food, when you chew once, you have to chew again next, between that when there is no chewing, find out the state of Rāma in the yogic way–there you will find it. Otherwise, you can find [Rāma] everywhere if you don't want to possess…

JOHN: So what does that mean, "find everywhere"? What's the technique for finding everywhere?

SWAMIJI: (laughs) I am lost.

JOHN: "In the universal way," this means?

SWAMIJI: Wherever you are, whatever you do, *bas*, you are in Rāma, no worry.

DENISE: So just stop worrying. Just go on doing everything you are doing and you'll find Him?

SWAMIJI: No, you *are* in Rāma, you are established in Rāma.

DENISE: But it's one thing to *be* in Rāma and to *know* you are in Rāma. If you think you're not, if you think you're away from it, from Him, then…no?

SWAMIJI: That is not Shaivism. Then you are not a Shaivite. You are just away from Shaivism. How can any other thing exist in the kingdom of God consciousness.

DENISE: It can't.

SWAMIJI: This is the kingdom of God consciousness, so God consciousness is flourishing everywhere, within and without: within the yogic state, without in the universal state.

DENISE: Well then why do most people miss Him if He is everywhere?

SWAMIJI: Missing is ignorance.

DENISE: But He's in ignorance, too.

SWAMIJI: You don't miss. How can you miss? How can you miss your life? You can't exist without That.

JOHN: But that's His trick also because He is my Self, so He misses, He's the one that does the missing.

SWAMIJI: He won't miss you.

DENISE: (laughs)

JOHN: No, but if there's only God in this world, only Lord Śiva exists in this world, then I am also only Lord Śiva. So if I miss Lord Śiva, that means He's missing Himself.

SWAMIJI: He's not missing. He's never missing. In the *Śivadṛṣṭi* he has explained–Somānanda:

Wisdom Verses 5 (28:46)

athocyate sarvadikke śivatattve vyavasthite /
tasmin jñāte'thavājñāte śivatvamanivāryatam //
(not recited in full)

Now I will explain to you Śiva, who is existing everywhere, within and without. *Tasmin jñāte'thavājñāte*, if you know Him, well and good; *athavā ajñāte*, if you don't know Him, well and good. *Śivatvamanivāryatam*, He is Śiva. If you know Him, He is there; if you don't know Him, He is still there, don't worry about it.

JOHN: No, but who does the knowing? Lord Śiva is knowing Himself.

SWAMIJI: If you know Him, that is good. If you don't know Him, that is also more than knowing–if you don't know Him. How can He be absent (laughs)? This is the philosophy of Somānanda, the master of Utpaladeva, the great grandmaster of Abhinavagupta. *Bas*, we will do only this much. *Bas*?

JOHN: Yes. In those earlier verses, we had those problems. Many problems were going to confront that person just at that point of *ekāgra*, the ending of *ekāgra*, before that *niruddha* state has dawned. Many obstacles come, ten thousand *lakh*s times one thousand.

SWAMIJI: Yes.

JOHN: Then you said there was going to be some relief. Where is that? That relief, we haven't come to that verse about relief.

SWAMIJI: Huh?

JOHN: You said there would be some relief.

DENISE: From all those obstacles.

JOHN: There is some relief. In other words, all these obstacles come, so many obstacles,…

SWAMIJI: Yes.

JOHN:…then you said that now we were going to speak about relief from those obstacles, but we haven't spoken about relief from those obstacles yet.

SWAMIJI: But we have spoken.

DENISE: What's the relief? That Rāma is in everything?

SWAMIJI: Yes, Rāma is everything.

DENISE: And that suffering and…

JOHN: But what are the obstacles? Aren't these the obstacles of these yogic powers and things that stand in your way?

SWAMIJI: Obstacles are…this is an obstacle: "I don't realize God. What shall I do? (Swamiji pounds his chest) What shall I do?" This is an obstacle. Why should you beat your chest? Nothing has happened to you if you realize it properly. How can God be excluded? He includes everything. This is an obstacle.

DENISE: To think, "I haven't realized God."

SWAMIJI: "I haven't realized God."

JOHN: These obstacles come all along or only at that point he's talking here?

SWAMIJI: Yes.

JOHN: All along or only at that point?

SWAMIJI: And still you don't believe (laughs), still you don't believe, although there is no meaning in not believing.

JOHN: There's no meaning in not believing.

SWAMIJI: (laughs) It is meaningless not to believe.

JOHN: Still there's no…I don't understand. It's meaningless not to believe, and yet still I don't believe. I don't quite understand.

SWAMIJI: It has no meaning not to believe.

DENISE: Not to believe what?

SWAMIJI: That, "I am not God, I am away from God." Thinking this way, this is called that *vighna* (obstacle).

DENISE: That's an obstacle.

SWAMIJI: That is obstacle.

JOHN: So all those are obstacles that come along the whole way of the path.

SWAMIJI: Yes.

JOHN: Not just at the end point. They are all along this path–these obstacles.

SWAMIJI: Yes.

JOHN: And those obstacles are mainly because you think that you are away from God.

SWAMIJI: But Somānanda says, "If there are obstacles, if there are not obstacles, what then? He is there." This is the only real way of understanding. How can you live without God consciousness? How can you exist? How can you talk without God consciousness? How can you remain dumb without God consciousness?

JOHN: He makes you dumb.

SWAMIJI: No. "He makes," no. Everything is there. Everything is there. He does not exclude anything. Nothing is excluded. His presence is included, His absence is included in His presence.

JOHN: In His absence, His presence is included?

SWAMIJI: Both.

JOHN: So when I think a thought, that's God thinking that thought, that's God's thought.

SWAMIJI: There are not two.

JOHN: No?

SWAMIJI: There are not two.

JOHN: There is only God's thought.

SWAMIJI: (Swamiji signals "what else?")

JOHN: So when you get to this state where you can't keep your mind focused, that's God's play.

SWAMIJI: That is not God's play. That is the position of God.

JOHN: That's not something else happening, that's actually…

SWAMIJI: That's actually another phase of God. He has got so many phases in this world. Ignorance is one, knowledge is one…

JOHN: And those are the same from the point of view of God? Ignorance and knowledge are the same thing. Nothing is better, you can't say this is better than that.

SWAMIJI: No "better," there is no "better."

JOHN: It doesn't work.

DENISE: I like that.

JOHN: So this whole section on Rāma, isn't this from the first *āhnika* of the *Tantrāloka*?

SWAMIJI: Yes, the first *āhnika*.

JOHN: When he talks about Rāma and he talks about Bhairava also in that same…

SWAMIJI: Yes, this is about Rāma.

VIRESH: Why did Pārvatī ask Śiva what Rāma is when Śiva is Rāma?

SWAMIJI: She wanted to know…

VIRESH: Yes, but Rāma is Śiva.

SWAMIJI: Yes.

VIRESH: She knew Śiva so–She was married to Him–so why did She ask that question?

SWAMIJI: She puts question only for our…

VIRESH: Our play?

SWAMIJI: Just play.

VIRESH: Oh.

SWAMIJI: It is good that he puts questions. It seems that he needs to understand.

JOHN: We were talking today about God, because here in Kathmandu and so many places they show God as having so many forms, like Lord Śiva sitting with *candra* and they show the shapes of Bhairava and so forth. And so we were discussing these forms of God, and Viresh says that he thinks that God is only like air, he doesn't feel that He has any form. Can you say something about the form of God, whether God has forms or doesn't have forms, or what that means?

SWAMIJI: He has got universal forms, all forms are His forms, you can't exclude any form. This is His formation.

JOHN: Why do people make *mūrti*s then? What is the point of…? Why do people construct *mūrti*s with specialized forms? What is the purpose…?

SWAMIJI: Construct what?

JOHN: *Mūrti*s, forms of…

INDERJI: *Mūrti*s, with specialized forms, suppose, Lord Śiva.

SWAMIJI: But this monistic Śaivism does not…

JOHN: Recognize that.

SWAMIJI:…recognize that–*mūrti*s.

JOHN: So these are from dualistic or mono-cum-dualistic schools.

SWAMIJI: Yes. Here, in Kathmandu you'll find the mono-dualistic way of the exposition of Śaivism, not monistic Śaivism. Monistic Śaivism is only in northern India. [Nepal] is just eastern India.

INDERJI: (Hindi) What is the explanation about this?

SWAMIJI: *Mūrti mana.* This is also fine in its own way.

JOHN: *Mūrti*s.

SWAMIJI: Yes.

JOHN: But if you think that's the real thing, then that's limiting.

If you think that God is only in this way,…

SWAMIJI: Only, no.

JOHN:…then you get limited.

SWAMIJI: It is not "only" this.

JOHN: So a Śiva *liṅga* is a more universal form of God? I mean, in your mind, thinking?

SWAMIJI: Śiva *liṅga* is better than a *mūrti*…

JOHN: Better than *mūrti*.

SWAMIJI:…because it has no form.

JOHN: No face, you mean; no body, no…it's only a God-idea.

SWAMIJI: Yes.

Wisdom Verses 5 (39:11)

MOKṢASYA LAKṢAṆAM
THE DEFINITION OF LIBERATION

JOHN: Ready, Sir.

SWAMIJI:

न मोक्षो नभसः पृष्टे न पाताले न भूतले ।
सर्वाशासंक्षये चेतः क्षयो मोक्ष इतीष्यते ॥५९॥
(इति वेदान्ते)

na mokṣo nabhasaḥ pṛṣṭe na pātāle na bhūtale /
sarvāśāsaṁkṣaye cetaḥ kṣayo mokṣa itīṣyate //59//

Now he says the tradition [of] what is *mokṣa* (liberation), the tradition according to the statement of Vedānta and the tradition according to the statement of Trika *āgama*. Both are given here. First is the tradition of, the definition of *mokṣa* according to the tradition of Vedānta. You must calculate that. (Swamiji repeats the verse) *Mokṣa* is not, liberation is not found in *nabhasaḥ*, in the ether. If you search in the ether, you won't find *mokṣa* in the ether. *Pṛṣṭhe*, you won't find *mokṣa* behind yourself. *Na pātāle*, you won't find *mokṣa* in *pātāl*. You know *pātāl*? *Pātāl* is the underworld, in the place which is situated [in the] underworld. There also you won't find *mokṣa*. Then what is *mokṣa* then? He says, *sarvāśāsaṁkṣaye*, when all *vikalpa*s (thoughts) take their end, and *cetaḥ kṣaye*, and the mind becomes one-pointed, *mokṣa itīryate*, that is *mokṣa*. It is *mokṣa* defined in Vedānta.

JOHN: And this verse comes from where, Sir?

SWAMIJI: This verse comes from Vasiṣṭha. Vasiṣṭha is the perfect course of Vedānta.

JOHN: *Yoga Vasiṣṭha*.

SWAMIJI: *Yoga Vasiṣṭha*, yes, the big one. Now it is in Trika *āgama*, what is the definition of *mokṣa*.

JOHN: From where is this from, Sir? This one is from Trika *āgama*?

SWAMIJI: Yes, Trika *āgama*. It is from Abhinavagupta's *Paramārthasāra*. You know the *Paramārthasāra* of Abhinavagupta?

JOHN: Yes, Sir.

SWAMIJI: Yes. In that *Paramārthasāra*, this *śloka* is quoted by Abhinavagupta:

Wisdom Verses 5 (44:05)

मोक्षस्य नैव किञ्चिद् धामास्ति न चापि गमनमन्यत्र ।
अज्ञानग्रन्थभिदा स्वशक्त्यभिव्यक्तता मोक्षः ॥ ६० ॥

mokṣasya naiva kiñcid dhāmāsti na cāpi gamanamanyatra /
ajñānagranthabhidā svaśaktyabhivyaktatā mokṣaḥ //60//

Mokṣasya naiva kiñcit dhāmāsti, actually *mokṣa* has no place where you will find it. It is not placed somewhere at some particular place. *Na cāpi gamanamanyatra*, you have not to go anywhere to find *mokṣa*. Wherever you are seated, you can liberate your Self there.[26] Or you can

26. "For attaining *mokṣa*, you have not to tread [away] from the state where you are already existing in the field of *māyā*. You are existing in the field of *māyā*, and you have to get elevated by-and-by, by-and-by, by *abhāysa* (practice), but you have not

liberate yourself, *ajñāna grantha bhidā*, when all knots of ignorance are shattered to pieces–all knots, all bindings, all limitations of entanglements, involvements, are shattered. And *svaśakty-abhivyaktatā*, and [when] your energies come into force, into action, into the fullness of activity, that is *mokṣa*; [when] *cit śakti*, *ānanda śakti*, *icchā śakti*, *jñāna śakti*, and *kriyā śakti* come into fullness of manifestation, that is *mokṣa*.[27] When *cit śakti*, *ānanda śakti*, *icchā śakti*, *jñāna śakti*, and *kriyā śakti*, all these five energies are covered with your own *vṛtti*s of mind (movements of mind), then *mokṣa* is not seen, it is not felt at all.

JOHN: So *vṛtti* means what? Modifications or…?

SWAMIJI: *Vṛtti* means, just the flux of mind, the flux of *vikalpa*s (thoughts). When *vṛtti* is found in the flux of *vikalpa*s, that is bondage. When the flux of *vikalpa*s have changed its position in *cit śakti*, *ānanda śakti*, *icchā śakti*, *jñāna śakti*, and *kriyā śakti*, these five *śakti*s, it is *mokṣa*.

JOHN: What does it mean to say "it has changed its position"? I'm confused.

SWAMIJI: Position. Position is that as long as you are a slave to your *vṛtti*s, as long as you remain a slave to your thoughts, a slave to your flux of mind; wherever you think, "I'll do this, I'll do this, I'll do this," as long as you do this job, you are entangled in this world, there is no possibility of attaining *mokṣa*. As long as you shun all these and your energies get manifested perfectly, that is *mokṣa*–all the five energies. That is what he says here.

Wisdom Verses 5 (48:03) end
Wisdom Verses 6 (00:15) start

It is the Trika *āgama* according to the theory of Abhinavagupta. Now *mokṣa*, the definition of *mokṣa* according to the theory of the Tantras.

JOHN: Could you sing that previous verse one more time please, Sir?

SWAMIJI:

---

to tread, there is no journey to be covered. The starting point of the journey is the ending point of the journey." *Paramārthasāra*, 60.

27. *Cit śakti* (energy of consciousness), *ānanda śakti* (energy of bliss), *icchā śakti* (energy of will), *jñāna śakti* (energy of knowledge), *kriyā śakti* (energy of action).

mokṣasya naiva kiñcid dhāmāsti na cāpi gamanamanyatra /
ajñānagranthabhidā svaśaktyabhivyaktatā mokṣaḥ //60//

Right?

JOHN: Yes, Sir. Thank you.

SWAMIJI: Now another *śloka* for *mokṣa*, and this *mokṣa* is according to the theory of the Tantras. That *mokṣa* was according to the theory of Abhinavagupta.

Wisdom Verses 6 (01:26)

मोक्षो हि नाम नैवान्यः स्वरूपप्रथनं हि सः ।
स्वरूपं चात्मनः संविन्नान्यत्तत्र तु याः पुनः ॥६१॥
क्रियादिकाः शक्तयस्ताः संविद्रूपाधिका नहि ।
असंविद्रूपतायोगाद्धर्मिणश्चानिरूपणात् ॥६२॥
(युगलकं)

mokṣo hi nāma naivānyaḥ svarūpaprathanaṁ hi saḥ /
svarūpaṁ cātmanaḥ saṁvinnānyattatra tu yāḥ punaḥ //61//
kriyādikāḥ śaktayastāḥ saṁvidrūpādhikā nahi /
asaṁvidrūpatāyogāddharmiṇaścānirūpaṇāt //62//

It is *yugalakam* (*yugalakam* means two *śloka*s making one sentence).

JOHN: Do you know which Tantra this comes from, Sir?

SWAMIJI: It is quoted by Abhinavagupta in the *Tantrāloka* (1.155-56). *Mokṣo hi nāma naivānyaḥ*, *mokṣa* is not something separate that you have to find. *Mokṣa* is just *svarūpa prathanaṁ*, just the realization of your own nature. But what is the nature? What is the position of nature? He defines now: *Svarūpaṁ ca ātmanaḥ saṁvit*, nature is one's own *saṁvit*; *saṁvit* means, one's own…how can I explain it?

VIRESH: Creation?

SWAMIJI: No, not one's own creation. It is *svarūpaṁ ca ātmanaḥ saṁvit*, your own understanding, your own understanding is *svarūpa*.

When you understand the position of your own nature, that is *svarūpa*. When you understand your nature as your mind...There are two phases of *svarūpa*: one is extroverted *svarūpa* (extroverted phase), another is the introverted phase. The extroverted phase is that of the mind, when there are thoughts, and it is a junk of thoughts. When you find in your nature a junk of thoughts, that is the extroverted phase of *svarūpa*. That is mind, that is no *svarūpa*. When it is introverted *svarūpa*, then you find the thought-less state, one-pointedness. That is the reality of your own nature. *Svarūpaṁ ca ātmanaḥ saṁvit*, your own nature of your own Self is *svarūpa*, *nānyat*, nothing else. *Svarūpa* is just the nature of your Being, the actual position of your Being.

JOHN: What is the literal meaning of *saṁvit*?

SWAMIJI: Literal meaning of *saṁvit* means, knowledge, pure knowledge, knowledge of your Self-knowledge.

JOHN: So *saṁvit-prakaśa* sometimes they say.

SWAMIJI: What?

JOHN: *Saṁvit-prakaśa* means that knowledge of your own awareness.

SWAMIJI: Samvit Prakāśa in Delhi (laughs). No, not that. *Svarūpaṁ ca ātmanaḥ saṁvit*, *svarūpa* is your own knowledge, knowledge of your own Self.

JOHN: Self-knowledge.

SWAMIJI: Self-knowledge is *svarūpa*, *nānyat*, nothing else–only Self-knowledge.[28] When Self-knowledge comes in its full manifestation, that is *svarūpa*. When Self-knowledge is smashed by the continuous flux of thoughts, it is gone, there is no *svarūpa*, *svarūpa* is absolutely absent. In place of *svarūpa* shines your mind with the flux of thoughts. In [Kṣemarāja's] *Pratyabhijñāhṛdaya*, it is also said in its *sūtra* in the *Pratyabhijñāhṛdaya* (*sūtra* 5):

citireva cetanapadādavarūḍhā cetyasaṁkocinī cittam /

Ceti, consciousness, God consciousness, when it moves down and leaves aside its real state of God consciousness, that takes the formation

28. "Your nature is your own consciousness (*svarūpam cātmanaḥ saṁvit*), nothing else. Your own consciousness is your *svarūpa* (nature)." *Tantrāloka* 1.55 (LJA archive).

of mind. And by the grace of God, this position of mind, when again tries to get elevated and gets entry in the state of God consciousness, that becomes *citi*. Mind is no more in existence then. As long as mind is existing, there is no possibility of *citi* (God consciousness). As long as God consciousness is there, there is no room for the mind. These are two phases produced by one Being. One is extroverted, one is introverted. Mind is the actual position of your Self, but it is disturbed, in its disturbed position. When your *svarūpa* is in the disturbed position, remains in a disturbed position, that is the state of the mind. When your *svarūpa* remains in the undisturbed position, that is *citi*, that is God consciousness. There is one: either mind or God consciousness. As long as there is the kingdom of the mind, there is no hope of the kingdom of God consciousness. As long as the kingdom of God consciousness is there, there is no place for the kingdom of the mind. Either the kingdom of the mind or the kingdom of God consciousness.

JOHN: So "kingdom of mind" means that state where there is only limited thoughts.

SWAMIJI: Junk of thoughts.

JOHN: One thought after another, endless thoughts.

SWAMIJI: Yes, endless.

DENISE: But in the state of God consciousness, thoughts come, but they're…

SWAMIJI: No, no, no, in God consciousness…no, no, they don't come. They have no right to come, they have no room to come.

DENISE: But a person who is in God consciousness and in the world, don't they have to think a thought before they perform an action?

SWAMIJI: No, that thought is not thought. That thought is…

DENISE: Direct, right from God, it's just God's thought.

SWAMIJI: That is not thought.

DENISE: What is that?

SWAMIJI: That is a fountain, that is a fountain of…

DENISE: Bliss?

SWAMIJI:…bliss. You can't imagine unless you realize it, experience it.

JOHN: But a man in the world, he does…so we can't say that a man in God consciousness thinks.

SWAMIJI: No, there is no thought in that way.

JOHN: But he's in the world doing and acting and so many things?

SWAMIJI: But he is rolling in God consciousness, there is no worry about him. He can do everything, each and every act what an ordinary person, an ignorant person does. But for him, all is divine, all is lying in his nature (*svarūpa*).

DENISE: And only he knows that.

SWAMIJI: He knows.

DENISE: No one else knows.

JOHN: So thought is by its nature limited. The definition of thought is something that is limited.

SWAMIJI: What?

JOHN: A thought by its definition a limited thing.

SWAMIJI: Limited, yes.

JOHN: And since a man in God consciousness doesn't have limited anything, he doesn't have thoughts.

SWAMIJI: Unlimited thought is not thought, it is *nirvikalpa*. It is the state of your own nature where there is no limitation.[29]

Tatra tu yā punaḥ kriyādikāḥ śaktaya, and in that state of God consciousness, *cit śakti*, *ānanda śakti*, *icchā śakti*, *jñāna śakti*, and *kriyā śakti*, this action does not stop altogether there. All activity is there in God consciousness. That *kriyā*, that knowledge, that activity is there; the same activity, the same knowledge, and the same will (*icchā*, *jñāna*, and *kriyā*), it is there, but these three are not *saṁvid rūpādhikā nahi*, they are not separate from God consciousness. They don't live separate from God consciousness there in that state of God consciousness. Why? *Asaṁvidrūpatā yogāt*, because if God consciousness is not there, they

---

29. *Nirvikalpa* (thought-lessness). "In reality, everything, whatever exists, it is in the *nirvikalpa* state [where] you can't define anything. You can define only in the *vikalpa* state, in the cycle of *vikalpa*, e.g., when you say, "This is a specks cover." But it is not a specks cover in the real sense, in the state of God consciousness. It is just *nirvikalpa*. You can't say what it is, but it is! *Saṁketādi smaraṇam*, when you understand, "This is mine," "O, this was in my house and this is mine," this memory takes place in the *vikalpa* state, not the *nirvikalpa* state. And that *vikalpa* state cannot exist without *anubhavam* (consciousness), the *nirvikalpa* state. *Nirvikalpa* is the cause of all *vikalpa*s, the undifferentiated state is the cause of all *vikalpa*s. It is not something foreign. It is their life, it is the life of all *vikalpa*s." *Parātrīśikā Vivaraṇa* (LJA archives).

won't exist. The existence is supposed to be…the existence of *icchā śakti*, the existence of *jñāna śakti* and *kriyā śakti* is actually based on *svarūpa* (God consciousness). God consciousness is the life of everything, and he feels that, "I am life-full always." *Asaṁvidrūpatā yogāt dharmiṇaścā nirūpaṇāt*, and there is no *dharma* and *dharmi bhava*, the aspects and the aspect-holder [are] not separate there. Who is the aspect-holder? The Lord, God. God is the aspect-holder. He has got numberless aspects (aspects means *dharma*s). For instance, *cit śakti* is His aspect, *ānanda śakti* is His aspect, *icchā śakti* is His aspect, *jñāna śakti* is His aspect, and *kriyā śakti* is His aspect. Creation is His aspect; protection, destruction, revealing, concealing, they are His aspects. But all these aspects are not separate from the aspect-holder there. This is the dualistic thought when people think that aspects and the aspect-holders are separate from each other. Aspects and the aspect-holder are one actually there in that real state of God consciousness.

JOHN: So this state of thought, in the definition of thought, people only [who are] acted have thoughts. In other words, you have taught us so many times that human beings that are in limited ignorance…

SWAMIJI: They are rolling in thoughts, they are just rolling in thoughts and they have…

JOHN: But they don't act.

SWAMIJI: No (affirmative).

JOHN: They're only act-…they're not act-…they don't act.

SWAMIJI: No, they are *acted.*

JOHN: Acted. So people that have thoughts are only acted. Thoughts are acted.

SWAMIJI: They are not actors.

JOHN: Actors don't have thoughts. It's *svātantrya.*

SWAMIJI: You have to become the actor, not the acted. You have to become the player, not the played.

JOHN: Everybody thinks that they are the player, but nobody is the player.

SWAMIJI: All are played as long as God consciousness is absent–they are played, they are not players. The player is he who plays, who controls what is played.

JOHN: *Svātantrya śakti.*

SWAMIJI: *Svātantrya śakti* is…

JOHN: So this *dharma* and *dharmi*, that's the oneness of Śiva and

Śakti, the aspect and the aspect-holder.

SWAMIJI: Aspect and aspect-holder. They are not separate in the state of Śiva. They are separated in the state of *jīva* (individuality), ignorance.

I have done these two *śloka*s, now another one:

Wisdom Verses 6 (15:35)

परमेश्वरशास्त्रे च न च काणाददृष्टिवत् ।
शक्तीनां धर्मरूपाणामाश्रयः कोऽपि कथ्यते ॥६३॥

parameśvaraśāstre ca na ca kāṇādadṛṣṭivat /
śaktīnāṁ dharmarūpāṇāmāśrayaḥ ko'pi kathyate //63//

In the Parameśvara *śāstra*, in Trika *śāstra*, you won't find [that] the manifestation of Śakti is found in aspects, the manifestation of Śiva is found in aspect-holders.

JOHN: You won't find that.

SWAMIJI: In Parameśvara *śāstra*, in Trika *śāstra*. In Trika *śāstra*, you won't find these separately. What?

DENISE: Śakti as the aspects and…

SWAMIJI: Śakti-aspects and the aspect-holder.

JOHN: Separate.

DENISE: Separate.

SWAMIJI: The aspects and the aspect-holder you won't feel separate, they are not separate there. Just like Kāṇāda, it is Kāṇāda's theory of understanding [that aspects and the aspect-holders are separate]. Kāṇāda was one *ṛṣi*. He was Lord Śiva's devotee, devotedly devoted to Lord Śiva, but he was an ascetic, he was performing penance, only doing this meditation on God. And he used to collect grains from *śali* land (rice fields). When *śali* was cut by those farmers and carried home, the remaining [grain that] was thrown there, left there, he would collect those *śali* grains for his livelihood for one year. He would soak it and eat a few grains each day. It was his job, it was his penance, and he was thinking of God only. Once, Pārvatī was with Śiva in a good mood, Śiva and Pārvatī were in a good mood, and Pārvatī asked Him,

"Why are You cruel to Your devotees? You have no sympathy for Your devotees." Pārvatī asked Śiva. Śiva said, "Whom have You seen that I have put cruelty on some devotee? Who is that devotee?"

JOHN: Śiva asked Pārvatī.

SWAMIJI: Śiva asked Pārvatī. Pārvatī said, "For instance, Kāṇāda. Kāṇāda *muni*, he devotes all his time in Your meditation and still his position is very tedious. He has to collect all the grains for his period of one year. Is this [how] You have bestowed him facility? Are You not cruel? He is Your devotee." [Śiva] said, "Don't think of him. He is a furious devotee. He will put Me in this [kind of] trouble that You cannot imagine. I am afraid of him. Don't touch him. Don't think of him. He is very furious." She said, "No, You are not...You are just talking, You are deceiving Me."

JOHN: Pārvatī says.

SWAMIJI: Pārvatī said. Then they both went there and Pārvatī appeared to [Kāṇāda] first. Śiva didn't dare to come near him first. Śiva told Pārvatī to see what his needs are. Pārvatī didn't ask what he needed. She said, "Lord Śiva has come to see you and your position. Are you quite happy?" He said, "Yes, I am quite happy. Has Śiva come here?" He asked Pārvatī. Then Pārvatī said, "Yes, Śiva wants to see you." "Please tell Him I want to see Him." Then He appeared there–Śiva. Kāṇāda told Him, "Are You pleased with me?" He said, "Oh, yes, I love you very much. I am pleased with you, with your penance and with whatever you do for Me. You meditate all the twenty-four hours." "Then please do one thing, please. You have come." [Lord Śiva] said, "What is your problem?" He said, "My problem is, it is tedious for me to collect these grains from the fields. Wherever I am situated, no grain must be produced so that I won't collect anything, I will sit in meditation." He asked this boon. (laughs) Then [Lord Śiva] abused Pārvatī and said, "You have put him in a worse condition now. He will have nothing to eat. See what You have done. This is [due to] Your asking Me again and again to help him." So wherever he was situated, no grain was produced in the...

JOHN: In that surrounding area.

SWAMIJI: In his area. [For] two miles, no grain, all was desert. It was made for him (laughs). And [Kāṇāda's] theory was *śakti*s and *śakti*-holders (aspects and aspect-holders) are separate. It was his theory of understanding. But Abhinavagupta says this is not the real theory what Kāṇāda *ṛṣi* held in his manner, so he gave a bullet to Kāṇāda *ṛṣi* (laughs). Because it is not like Śaivism [to say] that, "I won't take anything!" Why not take everything and remember God? What was there?

JOHN: That he had to not take anything? He was an ascetic, he didn't take anything.

SWAMIJI: Yes.

JOHN: For what point? So we don't believe that.

SWAMIJI: Śaivites don't believe that. Śaivites believe in, *bas*, enjoy wholeheartedly as much as you can, but don't miss God even for half a second. *Parameśvara śāstre ca na ca kāṇādadṛṣṭivat*, he is Kāṇāda; Kāṇāda means, who eats *kaṇu* (*kaṇu* means, grain). *Kaṇam atti eti kāṇāda*; *kaṇa* means those grains of *śali* (paddy). *Śaktīnāṁ dharmarūpāṇām āśrayaḥ ko'pi kathyate*, in the Trika *śāstra*, it is not said like that just like Kāṇāda was teaching his disciples [that] *śakti*s are separate and the holder of *śakti* is separate, they cannot be united, never can be united.[30]

Wisdom Verses 6 (24:46)

एक एव मनोदेवो जितः सर्वार्थसिद्धिदः ।
उन्यश्च विफलः क्लेशः सर्वेषां तज्जयं विना ॥६४॥

eka eva manodevo jitaḥ sarvārthasiddhidaḥ /
unyaśca viphalaḥ kleśaḥ sarveṣāṁ tajjayaṁ vinā //64//

Eka eva mano devo, when one's mind is controlled, *jitaḥ*, when you conquer the position of the mind, *sarvārtha siddhidaḥ*, what boons does it not bestow to you then afterwards–this mind? This mind becomes the producer of all boons to you if it is perfectly got under control. *Anyaśca viphalaḥ kleśaḥ sarveṣāṁ tajjayaṁ vinā*, if you have not conquered your mind, everything else in this world becomes useless, it is absolutely baseless and useless, nothing comes out of it. When you control your

30. "We recognize that all these aspects are one with that aspect-holder." *Tantrāloka* 1.157 (LJA archive).

mind, everything is there, everything you will achieve. If your mind is controlled, you can do whatever you like in this world. You have not to be the victim of threats of "This is to be done," "This is not to be done," "Oh, you should not do this, you should not do this." There is not that distinction afterwards. Afterwards, no distinction remains when your mind is under control, it has come under control.

Now in the next *śloka*s, there are, for instance, the one who is situated in *anupāya* (one master who is situated in *anupāya*, not *śāmbhavopāya*, not *śāktopāya*, not *āṇavopāya*), who is established in the *anupāya* state, for him, it is not possible for him to initiate those whose mind is inferior, inferiorly established in the lower fields, for instance, in *śāktopāya*, in *śāmbhavopāya*, and in *āṇavopāya*. Those yogis who are fit for *śāmbhavopāya*, who are fit for *śāktopāya*, and who are fit for *āṇavopāya*, those yogis are not elevated by the yogi who is established in *anupāya*. You understand what is *anupāya*? *Anupāya* is…

DENISE: It is beyond *śāmbhavopāya*.

SWAMIJI: Yes.[31]

Wisdom Verses 6 (28:52)

सोऽपि स्वातन्त्र्यधाम्ना चेदप्यनिर्मलसंविदाम् ।
अनुग्रहं चिकीर्षुस्तद्भाविनं विधिमाश्रयेत् ॥ ६५ ॥

so'pi svātantryadhāmnā cedapyanirmalasaṁvidām /
anugrahaṁ cikīrṣustadbhāvinaṁ vidhimāśrayet //65//
(not recited)

So'pi svātantryadhāmnā cet, for him, how he elevates his disciples who are fit for *anupāya*, those disciples who are fit for the state of *anupāya*, holding and understanding the state of *anupāya* (*anupāya*,

31. *Anupāya* is no *upaya* (no means). *Śāmbhavopāya* is the means pertaining to the energy of will (*icchā*). *Śaktopāya* is the means pertaining to the energy of knowledge or cognition (*jñāna*). *Āṇavopāya* is the means pertaining to the energy of action (*kriyā*).

where there is no means to be adopted)? He has just to sit before him, that guru has to sit before him, and make him [remain] seated in front of him, and tell him to "look at me." The *anupāya* guru tells him, directs him to "just gaze on my face." That is all what the initiation is being done, *bas*, he has not to speak anything to him. [The disciple] sits before [the guru] with folded hands and gazes on his [guru's] face and he sits in the state of *anupāya* himself–the guru. In the same way, he also becomes an *anupāya* guru at once just as a candle is lit by another candle. The candle which is not lit yet, when you light the candle, that other candle gets the same formation of flame, there is no difference in the flame for both. In the same way, established in the *anupāya* state, that master, when he lights his disciple with a glance only, he becomes a master also. There is no difference between the master and the disciple. Or *bhujaṅgavat garala saṁkrama*, or if you don't like this example of this candle, the candle example, take the example of a cobra. When a cobra is in front of you, he blows his poison in you and you also become poisonous; by blowing poison in your body, your body is poisonous as the cobra is poisonous. There is no difference between this cobra and the body of that other person. In the same way, the *anupāya* guru and the *anupāya* disciple, they are one, they become one. *Bhujaṅgavat garala saṁkrama*, this poison is inserted in him just like *bhujaṅga*, by a cobra. When a cobra inserts poison in another person, he becomes the manifestation of a poisonous embodiment. Nobody can touch him [without] becoming poisonous. Just this example [of a cobra] or that example of a candle. There is no difference between the two candles. A difference does not remain between the two poisonous beings. This is the way how the yogi who is established in the *anupāya* state can elevate others through a glance only, he has not to initiate them. Only one glance is enough, sufficient for him. But this glancing activity cannot work on those who are with dirty minds. "Dirty-minded disciples" means those worthy of *śāmbhavopāya*, worthy of *śāktopāya*, and worthy of *āṇavopāya*. They cannot find any benefit from that master.

DENISE: He's too high for them.

SWAMIJI: They cannot understand it. Now he says, *so'pi*, and if that *anupāya* guru, if the *anupāya* guru wishes sometime, *svātantrya dhāmnā*, with his free will–it is not binding for him to elevate those disciples; only he has to elevate those who are absolutely pure, fit for *anupāya*–if he means to elevate those who are unfit for *anupāya*, elevate those in their own way (some in *śāmbhavopāya*, some in *śāktopāya*, some in *āṇavopāya*), then I direct those masters to read my *Tantrāloka*. They must go through my *Tantrāloka* and then they can initiate them. He has to respect the *Tantrāloka*, he has to understand the *Tantrāloka*, he has to read the *Tantrāloka* from other masters, for elevating them. Elevating whom?

JOHN: Disciples in the other three *upāya*s (means).

SWAMIJI: Yes.

JOHN: So the meaning of this verse then is?

SWAMIJI: *So'pi svātantryadhāmnā*, *svātantrya dhāmnā*, if he so wishes, *svātantrya dhāmnā*, by *svātantrya*, he wishes that, "I want to elevate those people also; I have elevated this [disciple] who was fit for *anupāya*, I have elevated him, [but] I want to elevate those also, with dirty minds," then he has to go and find a master who will teach him the *Tantrāloka*. This does not mean that by the teachings, by being taught by other masters, he will come down from the reality of *anupāya*. He won't come down from the reality of *anupāya*, but he cannot elevate them without knowing the inferior theory of ways. He must learn that inferior theory of ways.

Wisdom Verses 6 (36:35)

तदर्थमेव चास्यापि परमेश्वररूपिणः ।
तदभ्युपायशास्त्रादिश्रवणाध्ययनादरः ॥ ६६ ॥

tadarthameva cāsyāpi parameśvararūpiṇaḥ /
tadabhyupāyaśāstrādiśravaṇādhyayanādaraḥ //66//
(not recited)

Tadarthameva cāsyāpi, for them, *asyāpi parameśvara-rūpiṇaḥ*, although he is one with God, he is established in *anupāya*, *tadabhyupāya śāstrādi śravaṇādhyayanādaraḥ*, the means for them, that is the *Tantrāloka*. He has to read the *Tantrāloka*, he has to learn the *Tantrāloka*, and he has to respect the *Tantrāloka*, and he has to produce the theory of the *Tantrāloka* for them.

Now, there is doubt. A doubt comes in-between these two.[32] If he is established in *anupāya*, is it not a shame for him to go to another master to learn the *Tantrāloka*? If he is established in *anupāya*, is it not a shame? It is shameful for him. [Abhinavagupta] says, "No, it is not a shame."

Wisdom Verses 6 (37:43)

नहि तस्य स्वतन्त्रस्य क्वापि कुत्रापि खण्डना ।
नानिर्मलचित्तः पुंसोऽनुग्रहस्त्वनुपायकः ॥६७॥
(कुलकं)

nahi tasya svatantraśya kvāpi kutrāpi khaṇḍanā /
nānirmalacittaḥ puṁso'nugrahastvanupāyakaḥ //67//
(not recited in full)

He is *svātantrya* (independent)! For himself he has nothing to do. It is for others he has to develop. He has to go to masters and read the *Tantrāloka* for others, not for himself. He does not need the *Tantrāloka* to understand [for himself]. For others he has to understand the *Tantrāloka*. *Nānirmalacittaḥ puṁso'nugrahastvanupāyakaḥ*, *anupāyakaḥ anugraha* (the grace of *anupāya*) cannot be suitable for that person who is filled with dirt in his mind, so he has to read the *Tantrāloka* for him.

Now there is another *śloka*. It is the taste of God consciousness, whoever has experienced the taste of God consciousness.

---

32. Jayaratha's commentary states: *nanvevamupāyamukhaprekṣitvādasya svātantryahāniḥ*.

Wisdom Verses 6 (38:58)

अयं रसो येन मनागवाप्तः स्वच्छन्दचेष्टानिरतस्य तस्य ।
समाधियोगव्रतमन्त्रमुद्रा जपादिचर्या विषवद्विभाति ॥६८॥

ayaṁ raso yena manāgavāptaḥ svacchandaceṣṭāniratasya tasya /
samādhiyogavratamantramudrā japādicaryā viṣavadvibhāti //68//

Ayaṁ rasa, this kind of taste of *anupāya*, *yena manāgavāptaḥ*, he who has achieved this kind of taste of the *anupāya* state of God consciousness, *svacchanda ceṣṭāniratasya tasya*, he becomes free and he becomes perfectly *svatantra* (independent) just like Lord Śiva.[33] For him, to adopt *samādhi*, yoga (the practice of yoga), *vrata* (vows), fasting, mantra (recitation of mantras), *mudrā* (recitation of postures), *japādi caryā* (and reciting of *japa*), *viṣavat vibhāti*, all these things seem to him just like poison. He does not want to do these things afterwards. He has not to go in the state of *samādhi*, he has not to go in the state of yoga, he has not to recite mantra, he has not to remain in some particular posture of a yogic posture, or he has not to do any *japa*. All these things appear to him just like poison. What has he to do with these? For him, wherever he is situated, let him remain as he is.[34]

---

33. "This taste of internal Being, this taste of internal being of observing this whole universe as a reflection in the mirror of Consciousness, observing the thirty-six elements from a to z (that is, from Śiva to earth), that this whole universe is no other than my Being, and observing that from a to z this whole universe is only the expansion of I, I-being (*ahaṁ parāmārśa*), for that person, this *rasa* of these three ways, who has tasted only once, he becomes absolutely independent from all sides." *Tantrāloka* 3.269 commentary (LJA archive).

34. "He does not like it because he is absolutely attached in that supreme Being. He does not need it, but he has to do all these things also just to keep an example for others. That is what [Lord Kṛṣṇa] says. He has to do *pūja* (worship), he has to do *yajña*s (sacrifices), he has to do everything for the benefit of others, not for himself. If he hates it, internally he hates it, he does not like it, he has no liking for sitting like this, closed eyes, or doing breathing exercise, meditation, *dhyāna*, *vrata*,

Wisdom Verses 6 (41:50)

तत्त्वमात्मस्थमज्ञात्वा मूढःशास्त्रेषु मुह्यति ।
गोपः कुक्षिगतं छागं कूपे पश्यति दुर्मतिः ॥ ६९ ॥

tattvamātmasthamajñātvā mūḍhaḥ śāstreṣu muhyati /
gopaḥ kukṣigataṁ chāgaṁ kūpe paśyati durmatiḥ //69//
(not recited)

Really, this nature of God consciousness is within your own Self. *Tattvam ātmastham*, this reality of God consciousness, which is situated in your own nature, *ajñātvā*, you leave that aside, you don't find it properly. One who does not find properly the reality of God consciousness within his own nature [is] *mūḍhaḥ* (and that *mūḍhaḥ* means that duffer yogi). *Śāstreṣu muhyati*, he begins to read the *śāstra*s (scriptures), he begins to read the *śāstra*s to find out the reality of God consciousness, [but] he cannot find out the reality of God consciousness by reading *śāstra*s. It is just like *gopaḥ kukṣigataṁ chāgaṁ* (*gopaḥ* means the shepherd), *kukṣigataṁ chāgaṁ*, when a small baby sheep [that] he has in his lap, he carries the baby sheep in his lap, and [he] cries at the place near a well, he cries, "My baby sheep is drowned in the well." This is his misunderstanding, absolute misunderstanding. He sees the reflection of the baby sheep, which is actually situated in his lap, he sees the reflection of the baby sheep in the surface of the water in the well and thinks that in the well this baby sheep has been drowned. It is a misunderstanding. Just like this misunderstanding [that] he thinks that the baby sheep is [in the well], in the same way he misunderstands

---

everything, but he must do to teach others that you should do [these things] because they have not that capacity of residing in that supreme state of God consciousness. [Lord Kṛṣṇa] says, *buddhibhedaṁ na janayed*, this *buddhi bheda*, this secret, the truth of the secret you should not disclose to those people who are attached to *pūja*, who are attached to *havan*, who are attached to all these good things. You should not disclose that truth that it has no sense, it has no value. *Joṣayetsarva*, on the contrary, you should also do *pūja* with them." *Bhagavad Gītā* 3.26 audio (LJA archive).

his own Self, which is situated in his own nature, that this Self will come out by reading the *śāstras*. The *śāstras* won't reveal that Self to him. Do you understand? (Swamiji repeats the verse)

Wisdom Verses 6 (44:58)

बहिर्मुखस्य मन्त्रस्य वृत्तयो या प्रकीर्तिताः ।
ता एवान्तर्मुखस्यास्य शक्तयः परिकीर्तिताः ॥७०॥

bahirmukhasya mantrasya vṛttayo yā prakīrtitāḥ /
tā evāntarmukhasyāsya śaktayaḥ parikīrtitāḥ //70//

Bahir mukhasya mantrasya, *mantra* [which] is *bahir mukha*, extroverted, this *mantra*, when extroverted, it becomes, it takes the formation of *vṛtti*s. *Vṛtti*s means, for instance,…

DENISE: (inaudible)

SWAMIJI: No, *vṛtti*. *Vṛtti* means, for instance, seeing with the eyes, whatever is seen by the eyes, whatever is heard by the ears, whatever is smelt by the nose, whatever is felt by touch, whatever is spoken by the tongue, whatever is eaten by the mouth, the teeth, all these are *vṛtti*s of the mind. *Vṛtti*s means, the flux of the mind. They are called *vṛtti*s. As long as they are in the position of *vṛtti*s, they are to be ignored. They should get converted in *śakti*s (energies). As long as they are [extroverted] in the field of the objective world, they are *vṛtti*s. When they are diverted towards subjectivity, they become *śakti*s, they become energies.

In that theory of that seminar there in Gupta Ganga, they thought that the theory of Pratyabhijñā (Recognition) was these *indriya vṛtti*s (flux of the organs). I told them, *indriya vṛtti*s are separate and *śakti*s (energies) are separate. Energies are one-pointed, and as long as *vṛtti*s are concerned, they are not one-pointed, they are just the flux of the mind. You should not get established in the state of *vṛtti*s, one should get established in the state of *śakti*s. *Śakti* is *antar mukha* and *vṛtti* is *bahir mukha*.

JOHN: External and internal.

SWAMIJI: Yes. Internal is *śakti*. So you must live in *śakti*s, you must not live in *vṛtti*s.

JOHN: Why did they think Pratyabhijñā was *vṛtti*s?

SWAMIJI: They didn't understand it properly. (Kashmiri) This is the theory of Utpaladeva.

JOHN: *Vṛtti*s is only flux of the mind.

SWAMIJI: Yes. When the flux of the mind becomes un-minded, it is diverted in *śakti*s, they become the *śakti*s of Lord Śiva: *cit śakti*, *ānanda śakti*, *icchā śakti*, *jñāna śakti*, and *kriyā śakti* are there.

JOHN: So *śakti*s in this sense are what? *Śakti*s are the energies of Lord Śiva.

SWAMIJI: Yes, these are the energies of Lord Śiva.

JOHN: But how do they relate to *vṛtti*s?

SWAMIJI: As long as they are in the objective field, there are *vṛtti*s. When the objective field ends, they become *śakti*s (energies), and he becomes one with God consciousness. That is the meaning of this *śloka*. *Bahir mukhasya mantrasya vṛttayo yā prakīrtitāḥ*, *bahir mukha mantra*s have got *vṛtti* adjusted. *Antar mukhasya*, when he is introverted in his God consciousness, *śaktayaḥ parikīrtitāḥ*, they become *śakti*s, they become energies then, they take the position of [*śakti*s].

JOHN: So any *mantra*?

SWAMIJI: Any *mantra*.

JOHN: So you take any *mantra*, as long as you are thinking that *mantra* or having that *mantra* or saying [that *mantra*], that is *vṛtti*, on the level of *vṛtti*.

SWAMIJI: As long as it is on the level of *vṛtti*, it is extroverted, it is in the field of *jīva* (limited being). It must be diverted into *śakti*s, that is, *nirvikalpa* (thought-lessness).

JOHN: That is *paśyantī*.

SWAMIJI: Yes.

JOHN: That becomes *paśyantī vāk*.

SWAMIJI: Yes.

Wisdom Verses 6 (50:20)

हस्तं हस्तेन संपीड्य दन्तैर्दन्तांश्च पीडयन् ।
अङ्गान्यंगैर्समाक्रम्य जयेदादौ स्वकं मनः ॥७१॥

hastaṁ hastena saṁpīḍya dantairdantāṁśca pīḍayan /
aṅgānyaṁgairsamākramya jayedādau svakaṁ manaḥ //71//

So it is worthwhile for the aspirant to control [their] mind. You must control your mind. Whatever you will have to do, do that, do that and wholeheartedly control your mind. *Hastaṁ hastena saṁpīḍya* (*hastaṁ* means, squeeze your hands with your hands), with both of your hands, squeeze your hands [together] with force (*hastaṁ hastena saṁpīḍya*). *Dantair dantāṁśca pīḍayan*, squeeze your [upper] teeth with your other part of teeth, the lower part of teeth, like this (*dantair dantāṁśca pīḍayan*). *Aṅga anyaṁgair samākramya*, squeeze your limbs of the body with the other limbs of your body. *Jayed ādau*, control your mind, see that your mind is one-pointed.

JOHN: Where is this verse from?

SWAMIJI: Huh?

JOHN: These verses are from where?

SWAMIJI: You'll be angry. These verses are of Vedānta (laughs), but it is worthwhile to have it (laughs).[35]

DENISE: (laughs) It didn't sound like Śaivism.

SWAMIJI: [John] is very tough (laughs).

DENISE: Yeah.

SWAMIJI: It is why I appreciate [John]. He has got the Śaivite seed in him, he has digested that Śaivite seed. But it is worthwhile, you should do it (Swamiji repeats the verse). One must conquer this mind.

JOHN: So this is the only verse that was in Vedānta. This verse?

SWAMIJI: Yes.

JOHN: But not the others.

SWAMIJI: No, no, not the others.

Wisdom Verses 6 (53:37) end
Wisdom Verses 7 (00:00) start

Why not do one *śloka* first? One *śloka* we'll do. He goes to that *anupāya* state of the master.

---

35. "This is the advice of Vaśiṣṭhaḥ to Rāma." *Practice and Discipline* (LJA archive).

JOHN: Again, back to that one.
SWAMIJI: Yes.

तं ये पश्यन्ति ताद्रूप्यक्रमेणामलसंविदः ।
तेऽपि तद्रूपिणस्तावत्येवास्यानुग्रहात्मता ॥७२॥

taṁ ye paśyanti tādrūpyakrameṇāmalasaṁvidaḥ /
te'pi tadrūpiṇastāvatyevāsyānugrahātmatā //72//

Taṁ ye paśyanti tādrūpyakrameṇāmalasaṁvidaḥ, amala saṁvidaḥ, those whose God consciousness is so fine and who are liable to get entry at any moment in the state of *anupāya*, those disciples, when they *paśyanti* (look) on that master who is established in the *anupāya* state, *tadrūpya krameṇa*, by going deep, by going deep and thinking in which state he is established,…*

He thinks. Who? The disciple. The disciple imagines in his own mind at what stage he is established.

DENISE: His master is established.

SWAMIJI: Yes.

*…at that very moment, he becomes, he takes hold of that state at once. *Te'pi tadrūpiṇa*, they become not even less than [the master]. A little bit less also they don't [become]. They become one and the same like [their] masters. So they are *just* masters. *Te'pi tadrūpiṇas*, they become one with that *svarūpa* (nature) of the master. *Tāvatyeva*, this much, this much *anugraha* (grace) was needed for them, *bas*, that is all. They have been blessed by the master like this. No initiation, no *mantra*, nothing, bas, they are established forever in that *anupāya*. *Bas*, it is over now.

JOHN: That one, yes. Now we go to those verses from the *Rāmāyaṇa*.

SWAMIJI: *Rāmāyaṇa*, yes.

Wisdom Verses 7 (03:01)

Srīrāmaśabdasya Pāramārthikatvam
The Reality of the Word "Rāma"

पूर्णानन्दस्वभावः स्वजनहितकृते माययोपात्तकायः ।
कारुण्यादुद्दिधीर्षुर्जनमनवरतं मोहपङ्के निमग्नम् ॥७३॥

pūrṇānandasvabhāvaḥ svajanahitakṛte māyayopāttakāyaḥ /
kāruṇyāduddidhīrṣurjanamanavaratam̐ mohapan̐ke nimagnam //73//

It is "*ṣur*": *uddidhīr-ṣur*. '*Ra*' is omitted there.

आविश्यान्तरवसिष्ठं बहिरपि कलयन् शिष्यभावं वितेने ।
यः संवादेन शास्त्रामृत जलधिममुं रामचन्द्रं प्रपद्ये ॥७४॥

āviśyāntarvasiṣṭham̐ bahirapi kalayan śiṣyabhāvam̐ vitene /
yaḥ sam̐vādena śāstrāmṛta jaladhimamum̐ rāmacandram̐ prapadye //74//

I bow to that Rāmacandra, I bow to that embodiment of Lord Śiva (Rāmacandra), I bow to Him wholeheartedly. With heart and soul I bow to Him. Who was He? *Pūrṇānanda*…

The connection is, this is *yuglakam*: both *śloka*s have got only one verb, so it is one sentence in two *śloka*s.

…*pūrṇānanda svabhāvaḥ*, actually Rāma was the embodiment of complete full bliss, the completion of the extreme bliss of God consciousness (that is *pūrṇānanda svabhāvaḥ*). His *svarūpa* (nature) was just filled with divine ecstasy of God consciousness. If He was established in that stage, what was the need for Him to get birth in a physical body? *Svajana hitakṛte*, to elevate all the ignorant people existing in this universe. By His *svātantrya śakti* (energy of independence),

He adjusted His soul in a body, He appeared in a body for the upliftment of each and every being who were tossed by the kicks of *māyā* every now and then. For uplifting those, He held a body for Himself to manifest in this world. Otherwise He was filled with God consciousness always. *Kāruṇyāt uddidhīrṣur*, *kāruṇyāt*, by pity, by taking pity on those tortured living beings in this *saṁsāra* (their condition was pitiable), and by that pity He took pity on them. *Uddidhīrṣur janam*, He wanted to elevate those people to get rid from the *māyā* in which they were stuck and couldn't come out from this cycle of *māyā*. *Mohapaṅke nimagnam*, who were drowned in the *mohapaṅke* (*mohapaṅke* means that mud, the mud of ignorance of God consciousness, in that mud they were drowned), just to elevate them from that mud, He appeared in a body. Otherwise He was filled with God consciousness in His own way in heaven. Just to uplift those, He appeared in a body.

When He appeared in a body, then *āviśyāntar vasiṣṭhaṁ bahirapi kalayan śiṣya bhāvaṁ vitene*; *āviśyāntar vasiṣṭhaṁ*, He entered in Vasiṣṭha first. When He came in a body, after being established in His body, He entered in the consciousness of His master, and He became His master. The master was not separate from Rāma. Rāma entered in the body of the master and became the guru. *Bahirapi*, outwardly, *śiṣya bhāvaṁ*, outwardly He became His disciple as Rāma. Rāma was the same being, and His guru, Rāma's guru, was the same being, they were only one. He entered first in His master and then in the disciple, in Rāma. And *saṁvādena*, and put questions and answers, questions and answers, they manifested questions and answers. Questions were put by Rāma and answers would come from the lips of Vasiṣṭha. And really Vasiṣṭha was Rāma Himself. By the manifestation of these questions and answers in continuation, this *saṁvāda*, this talk, by developing this talk with each other, *śāstra amṛta jaladhim vitene*, He developed and manifested the *Yoga Vasiṣṭha*, a big *śāstra*. I bow to that Rāmacandra wholeheartedly, who did this for the upliftment of mankind.

This is the explanation of these two *śloka*s. Have you understood?

JOHN: Yes, Sir.

SWAMIJI: Now:

Wisdom Verses 7 (11:24)

गुरोर्वाक्याद्युक्तिप्रचयरचनोन्मार्जनवशात् ।
समाश्वासाच्छास्त्रं प्रतिसमुदिताद्वापि कथितात् ॥७५॥
विलीने शङ्काभ्रे हृदयगगनोद्भासिमहसः ।
प्रभोः सूर्यस्येव स्पृशत चरणान्ध्वान्तजयिनः ॥७६॥

gurorvākyādyuktipracayaracanonmārjanavaśāt /
samāśvāsācchāstraṁ pratisamuditādvāpi kathitāt //75//
vilīne śaṅkābhre hṛdayagaganodbhāsimahasaḥ /
prabhoḥ sūryasyeva spṛśata caraṇāndhvāntajayinaḥ //76//

The connection of these two *śloka*s is in one sentence. It is *yugalaka*, both *śloka*s.

Guror vākyāt, either by one word from the lips of a master, by one divine word from the lips of your master (this is one way of understanding)[36], or *yukti pracaya racana unmārjana vaśāt* (*yukti pracaya* means, by conducting the collection of the means), and by conducting the collection of so many means (*upāya*s), *unmārjana vaśāt*, by those means, when you smash all the impurities within your *ātma*, within yourself, *samā śvāsāt śāstraṁ prati*, or just take one important point from the *śāstra*s (scriptures) from the lips of your master, *bas*, that is sufficient to remove all your doubts,[37] *samuditāt vāpi kathitāt*, or by taking advice of the master in the formation of *śāmbhavopāya*, in the formation of *śāktopāya*, in the formation of *āṇavopāya*–all the three.

---

36. "For those [who are already purified], he has to speak only one word, *bas*: 'You are yourself God, nothing to be done. Don't do anything, you are yourself God,' and he becomes God. That one word is *anupāya*." *Tantrāloka* 2.49 (LJA archive).

37. "Your doubts that, 'I am not God consciousness, I am an individual, I am this body, I have got hands, I have got an appetite, I have got throat cancer, I have got a chest disease, I have got everything, I am fine,' these are the heaps of clouds in the vacuum of your mind, in the vacuum of your brain." Ibid.

At one place, he directs his disciple in *śāmbhavopāya*, other places he directs his disciple in *śāktopāya*, and at other places he directs his disciple on *āṇavopāya*. That is *samuditāt vāpi kathitāt*, when he takes the support of all the three *upāyas*. *Vilīne saṅkābhre*, when all doubts are removed by this way: *guror vākyāt*, by just one word, one supreme word from the master (that is *anupāya* first). If that does not work, then *yukti pracaya racana unmārjana vaśāt*, then you have to kick him down in *āṇavopāya*.

The theory of Abhinavagupta is that you should try the first *upāya* first. When any aspirant comes at your feet for the realization of God, you should tell him first *anupāya* because who knows which kind of *śaktipāta* (grace) he has been blessed with by Lord Śiva. He may be capable of *anupāya*, so try *anupāya* first. When *anupāya* does not work in him–that is *guror vākyāt*, one word from the master–if that does not work, then you should adopt the means of *āṇavopāya*. You should direct him to go absolutely down [and start] from the beginning, he should start from the beginning, from *āṇavopāya*. That is *yukti pracaya racana unmārjana vaśāt*, that is *āṇavopāya*, by conducting *āṇavopāya* to that disciple. Afterwards, when he is awakened by those *āṇavopāyas*, the collective means of *āṇavopāyas*, *samā śvāsāt śāstraṁ*, then the master should direct him and tell him the important points that are existing in the *śāstras* (that is *śāktopāya*). *Samuditāt vāpi kathitāt*, or *samuditāt vāpi kathitāt*, afterwards, *samuditāt vāpi kathitāt*, in a collective way he should advise him and initiate him (that is in *śāmbhavopāya*). First you should try *anupāya*, the guru should try to conduct *anupāya* first. If that does not work, then *āṇavopāya*. After *āṇavopāya*, you have to adopt *śāktopāya*. After *śāktopāya*, you have to adopt *śāmbhavopāya*. Then [the disciple] will be established fully in God consciousness. *Vilīne saṅkābhre*, his doubts will all be washed and his doubts will be cleaned, cleared, *hṛdaya gagana udbhāsi mahasaḥ*, in the ether of the heart, the sun of God consciousness will shine in his heart, in the ether of his heart, the sun of God consciousness will shine in its fullness. *Spṛśata*, let you touch the rays of that sun of God consciousness which are just to remove all the darkness of ignorance from all sides. You should do that.

This is advice for masters, it is not advice for disciples. Masters are advised to do this way the initiation to aspirants. First they should conduct *anupāya*. When that does not work, then *āṇavopāya*, the most inferior means he must adjust. And after those means are working–they will work because those are inferior means–after working out those means, he should push him ahead in *śāktopāya*. Then afterwards he should push him ahead in *śāmbhavopāya*. Ultimately, he'll be pushed in *anupāya* where the sun of God consciousness will shine in his heart in its fullness.

JOHN: Those two verses come from? That verse comes from? Those verses?

SWAMIJI: From the *Tantrāloka*.

JOHN: And that first verse about Rāma comes from?

SWAMIJI: It is from Vasiṣṭha, that big book of Vasiṣṭha. Now this is from some Tantra, this *śloka*, next.

JOHN: Seventy-four?

SWAMIJI: Seventy-four, yes.

Wisdom Verses 7 (20:45)

प्रज्ञाप्रासादमारुह्य अशोच्यः शोचतो जनान् ।
भूमिष्ठानिव शैलस्थः सर्वान्प्राज्ञोऽनुपश्यति ॥७७॥

prajñāprāsādamāruhya aśocyaḥ śocato janān /
bhūmiṣṭhāniva śailasthaḥ sarvānprājño'nupaśyati //77//

Just as in a plane, when you fly in a plane, when you reach the highest top and you are flying there, from there you look down below from the window and you'll see the town areas here and there,...*

You'll see town areas. For instance, you'll see this big hut. This big hut, where it is established, it is so big, [but] from there [in the airplane] you will find it [appears to be] this much [in size]. And people walking on the roadside, you will see this [tiny] height of people walking on the roadside (laughs). And a motorcar [appears] just [like] one top of a needle–this is that much big you find it. That is *prāsāda*.

*...when you reach at the stage of *prāsāda*, that top section of God consciousness, and you look down below [at] the position of worldly people, how they act in their own way (limitation),...*

Even big bungalows that cost thirty-five *lakh*s seems to be just this much [in size] from an aeroplane. That is what I felt when I was flying from Delhi to Kathmandu.

*...that is *prajñā prāsādam āruhya*, when he ascends that highest seat of *prajñā* (knowledge, God consciousness), *aśocyaḥ*, he becomes *aśocyaḥ*, he is all-blissful. Only depression comes when it falls down a little bit.

DENISE: He falls sometimes?

SWAMIJI: No, when the plane goes a little down, then depression. Otherwise, if it's going up and up, you find joy. Don't you find joy? You experience joy as much as it goes higher, higher, higher. That is *prāsāda*. *Prāsāda* means that highest elevated state. When you are situated in that highest elevated state of God consciousness, *aśocyaḥ*, you become *aśocyaḥ*, filled with joy. *Śocato janān*, and those people who are tossing here and there on the ground just in their own limited way, *bhūmiṣṭhān iva śailasthaḥ*, just like *bhūmiṣṭhān*, those who are situated on the Earth, on the surface of Earth, and the person who is situated on the top peak of a mountain and he looks down below and he realizes the pitiable condition of those people, *sarvān prājño anupaśyati*, that elevated soul, he believes and sees the position of the whole world that way, in that limited consciousness, and [as for] himself, he is filled with joy.

It is a good *śloka*. It is in the Tantras. Now in the next *śloka*, he gives the actual position of that person who is established in *anupāya*.

Wisdom Verses 7 (25:36)

अविकल्पपथारूढो येन येन पथा विशेत् ।
धरासदाशिवान्तेन तेन तेन शिवीभवेत् ॥७८॥

avikalpapathārūḍho yena yena pathā viśet /
dharāsadāśivāntena tena tena śivībhavet //78//
(not recited)

For that yogi who is established in *anupāya*, all *upāya*s (means) become *anupāya* for him. *Śāmbhavopāya* becomes *anupāya* for him. If he conducts with *śāmbhavopāya*, for him it is as good as *anupāya*.

If he conducts *śāktopāya*, it is just like *anupāya* for him. All *upāya*s become the same, take the same position of the *upāya*s.

Now, the actual position of these *upāya*s is, when you are established in *āṇavopāya*, you are always in *āṇavopāya*. If you conduct with *śāktopāya*, that will become *āṇavopāya* to you. If you think of *śāmbhavopāya* or *śāktopāya* or *anupāya*, you will think [about them], but [they] will be *āṇavopāya* for that person. When you go ahead another step…

JOHN: *Śāktopāya*.

SWAMIJI:…*śāktopāya*, then *āṇavopāya* is *śāktopāya* for you, *śāktopāya* is *śāktopāya* for you. *Āṇavopāya* takes the position of *śāktopāya* for him. And *śāmbhavopāya* takes the position of *śāktopāya* for him. *Anupāya* also takes the position of *śāktopāya* for him. Do you understand?

JOHN: So everything is seen through that state.

SWAMIJI: Which state?

JOHN: If you are in *śāktopāya*, then everything becomes *śāktopāya* no matter whether it is *āṇavopāya*, *śāmbhavopāya*, or *anupāya*.

SWAMIJI: Yes. And for the person who is established in *śāmbhavopāya*, all *upāya*s are *śāmbhavopāya* to him. *Āṇavopāya* becomes *śāmbhavopāya*, *śāktopāya* becomes *śāmbhavopāya*, *śāmbhavopāya* is already *śāmbhavopāya*, and *anupāya* is *śāmbhavopāya* for him. And for the person who is established in *anupāya* (the highest *upāya*), for him everything is *anupāya*! He does not recognize any other *upāya* than *anupāya* everywhere. If he recites *mantra*s also, if he begins to breathe in and out and does this "*so'ham*," or all these *upāya*s, or *cakrodāya*, it becomes *anupāya* for him. This is the reality of these *upāya*s. *Avikalpapathārūḍho*–that is what he explains here–*avikalpathārūḍho*, the one who is established in *avikalpapath* (*avikalpapath* means, that *nirvikalpa* (thought-less) state, absolute *nirvikalpa* state, who is established in that state), *yena yena pathā viśet*, through any way he may tread, he may take a journey in any way, he may take the journey through *āṇavopāya*, he may take the journey through *śāktopāya*, he may take the journey through *śāmbhavopāya*, or he may take the journey through *anupāya* (*yena yena pathā*), *viśet dharā sadāśivāntena*, no matter if it is the state of *pṛthvī* (earth) element, or the state of Paramaśiva, *tena tena śivī bhavet*, all means become to him just *anupāya* (the superlative degree). This is the greatness of *anupāya*. At that stage:

Wisdom Verses 7 (29:51)

यथास्थितः तथैवास्व मा गाः बाह्यमथान्तरम् ।
केवलं चिद्विकासेन विकारनिकराञ्जहि ॥७९॥

yathāsthitaḥ tathaivāsva mā gāḥ bāhyamathāntaram /
kevalaṁ cidvikāsena vikāranikarāñjahi //79//

This *śloka* is penned down by Abhinavagupta himself in the *Bhairava Aṣṭaka*. There is the *Bhairava Aṣṭaka*, eight *śloka*s he has penned down in his own manner. This is one of those *śloka*s.

Yathāsthitaḥ tathaivāsva, wherever you are established, remain there, don't worry to move from that place wherever you are situated. *Mā gā bāhyam*, don't go outside or don't go up or don't go down, remain wherever you are established already. *Kevalaṁ cidvikāsena*, you have to enlighten the light of God consciousness, *vikāra nikarāñjahi*, then you will find God consciousness everywhere shining. You'll become blissful for all times.

Wisdom Verses 7 (31:21)

अर्थेषु तद्भोगविधौ तदुत्थे दुःखे सुखे वा गलिताभिशङ्कम् ।
अनाविशन्तोऽपि निमग्नचित्ताः जानन्ति वृत्तिक्षयसौख्य-
मन्तः ॥८०॥

artheṣu tadbhogavidhau tadutthe duḥkhe sukhe vā galitābhiśaṅkam /
anāviśanto'pi nimagnacittāḥ jānanti vṛttikṣayasaukhyamantaḥ //80//

Artheṣu, in the field of the objective world, *tat bhoga vidhau*, in the cognition of the objective world, *tadutthe duḥkhe sukhe vā*, in the field of its pain and pleasure, *galitābhiśaṅkam anāvīśanto'pi nimagna cittā*, those whose mind is absolutely focused in God consciousness, let them remain in the objective world, let them remain in the experiencing stage of the objective world, let them remain crying in pleasure and pain of the objective world. *Anāvīśanto api*, they are actually away from that! They are in that state, they are crying because of pain, they are happy when they are joyous, when they are in a happy mood, but their mind is absorbed in God consciousness altogether, for good. So, no matter whatever they are doing with respect to observers outside…they observe that, "They are like us, the same way, filled with…when they are pained, they are filled with sadness; when they are experiencing joy, they are filled with joy." In the same way, people observe them as they are existing in this world. They think, "They are just like us," but they are not actually. They are doing the same thing as ordinary people will do, but their mind is absolutely focused in God consciousness. No matter if they cry at the time of pain, no matter if they are happy at the time of pleasure, when they are excited also, it doesn't matter, they are actually established in God consciousness for always. So there will be no difference between…a difference cannot be marked in them by ordinary people, worldly people. Ignorant people cannot mark the difference, what difference they have got in connection with ordinary people. They feel, "They are just like us," [because] they are crying like them. (Swamiji repeats the verse) Actually, they are not soaked in that pain and pleasure at all, but from the viewpoint of ordinary, these worldly people, they seem to be soaked in the pain and pleasure of the world. Actually they are *nimagna cittāḥ*, their mind is absorbed in God consciousness in fullness. *Jānanti vṛtti kṣaya saukhyam*, they experience the fullness of ecstasy in each and every step of the world. In each and every movement of the world, they experience the state of the fullness of God consciousness.

Abhinavagupta has said in this *Parātrīṁśikā*: *duḥkhe'pi pravikāsena*,[38] in pain also you'll see the glamour of God consciousness, what to speak of pleasure? Pleasure is already the glamour of God consciousness. In pain also, in acute pain which is unbearable pain, there also you will find the gratitude of God consciousness. You won't find that pain separate from that God consciousness.

Now the question arises: Why should we explain in the collection of the *upāyas*, in the collection of these means, inferior means, in the

38. From Somānanda's *Śivadṛṣṭi* 5-9 as quoted in the *Parātrīśikā Vivaraṇa*.

masses of inferior means, why should we give reference of the means that is above the means–*anupāya*? He says another *śloka* for that:

Wisdom Verses 7 (38:44)

अनुत्तरेऽभ्युपायोऽत्र ताद्रूप्यादेव वर्णितः ।
ज्वलितेष्वपि दीपेषु घर्मांशुः किं न भासते ॥८१॥

anuttare'bhyupāyo'tra tādrūpyādeva varṁitaḥ /
jvaliteṣvapi dīpeṣu gharmāṁśuḥ kiṁ na bhāsate //81//

Anuttare abhyupāyo atra; *atra*, in the field of the inferior staff of means (that is, beginning from *śāmbhavopāya*, *śāktopāya*, and *āṇavopāya*, and all those *mantra*s and rituals and everything, all these *upāya*s which are established in the inferior surface of God consciousness), there I have nominated the position of *anupāya* also. But how it could be possible? It was not worth explaining there in that inferior place of God consciousness. I have explained it–Abhinavagupta says–I have explained it in the inferior state of God consciousness, in *śāktopāya*, in *śāmbhavopāya*, in *āṇavopāya* I have explained the state of *anupāya*. Why I have stated? *Jvaliteṣvapi dīpeṣu*, if candles are lit, no matter if the sun also rises, [the light of] candles will subside in their own way, they won't be perceived by anybody–candles, the light of candles. When the sun is rising, what is the position of candles? Candles can shine in their own way, let candles also shine, but they won't shine. That light of the sun will supersede all those lights. So there is no harm if *anupāya* is shining everywhere. *Jvaliteṣvapi dīpeṣu*, if *dīpeṣu* (candles) are *jvaliteṣvapi*, already lit, *gharmāṁśuḥ kiṁ na bhāsate*, is there no room for the rise of the sun there at that time moment? The sun can rise also.

JOHN: So *anupāya* is the sun.

SWAMIJI: *Anupāya* is the sun, yes (laughs). Sunshine is *anupāya*.

JOHN: So the candles then would be?

SWAMIJI: *Śāktopāya*, *śāmbhavopāya*, *āṇavopāya* and *mantra*s and rituals and all that nasty *bakwas* (nonsense).

JOHN: If the reality of God is only one and that everything is only

God, then why do we also worship and say *mantras* in praise of Lord Hanumān and Gaṇeśa and Pārvatī?

SWAMIJI: It is because we are not worthy for that for always. You cannot touch *anupāya* for always, you have to learn *anupāya*. You have not to practice on *anupāya* yet. When you master *śāmbhavopāya*, then you have the right to get entry in *anupāya* practice.

JOHN: So then who is Gaṇeśa and who is Hanumān?

SWAMIJI: Internally?

JOHN: Yes.

SWAMIJI: Lord Hanumān is the divine being of the doorkeeper. He is next to Gaṇeśa. Gaṇeśa is also a doorkeeper, and that is breath.

JOHN: Breath. So what is external Gaṇeśa? Is he the son of Lord Śiva? How are we to understand the external Gaṇeśa?

SWAMIJI: As the production of Śiva, Śiva's *svātantrya*.

JOHN: So one aspect of Śiva's *svātantrya* is the form of His son, Gaṇeśa. We think of him as this Gaṇeśa. And also another form is the…

SWAMIJI: Internal form…

JOHN: Internal form. The same with Lord Hanumān…

SWAMIJI: Yes. That is subtle.

JOHN:…he has an external form, too. And so externally he is known to be that form of…

SWAMIJI: External is also quite correct.

JOHN: So externally, Lord Hanumān is known for what? What does he do for his devotees? What does he…?

SWAMIJI: He guides, he guides at the time of entry.

JOHN: And Gaṇeśa, he does what for his devotees–external Gaṇeśa?

SWAMIJI: External Gaṇeśa also guides. Hanumān guides outwardly and external Gaṇeśa guides internally. In the cycle of breathing in and out, this is the kingdom of Hanumān. At that junction point is the kingdom of Gaṇeśa.

JOHN: So then, those devotees who worship Śakti, they worship Śakti as the means to attain Lord Śiva?

SWAMIJI: Yes. Śakti is the means.

JOHN: Because Śakti is in action.

SWAMIJI: *Anuttare'bhyupāyo'tra tādrūpyādeva varṅitaḥ*, the *upāya* of *anuttara*[39] (that is, *śāmbhavopāya*), *tādrūpyāt eva varṇita*, there is no harm if we explain the glamour of *śāmbhavopāya* in the explanation of *āṇavopāya* also–there is no harm. *Jvaliteṣvapi dīpeṣu*, where lies the harm if candles are lit and the sun also rises? There is no harm on that also.

Wisdom Verses 7 (45:35)

ततोऽपि परमं ज्ञानमुपायादिविवर्जितम् ।
आनन्दशक्तिविश्रान्तमनुत्तरमिहोच्यते ॥८२॥

tato'pi paramaṁ jñānamupāyādivivarjitam /
ānandaśaktiviśrāntamanuttaramihocyate //82//

Tato'pi paramaṁ jñānam, besides *śāmbhavopāya*, there is another supreme [means]–you can't say “supreme way/means,” it is not a means but it is a supreme stage, more supreme than *śāmbhavopāya*–*upāyādi vivarjitam*, where there is nothing to be done, no means are to be adopted there, and that stage is *ānanda śakti viśrāntam*, it resides in *ānanda śakti* (the energy of bliss) of God consciousness. *Anuttaram ihocyate*, it is one with *anuttara*, it is one with *cit śakti* (the energy of Consciousness).

So *cit śakti* and *ānanda śakti* are representative of, they indicate, *anupāya*. *Icchā śakti* indicates *śāmbhavopāya*, *jñāna śakti* indicates *śāktopāya*, and *kriyā śakti* indicates *āṇavopāya*. And *anupāya* is no *upāya*, it is the stage of Lord Śiva Himself (that is *ānanda śakti* and *cit śakti*). In *ānanda śakti* and *cit śakti* is the residence of *anupāya* where there is nothing to be done, no means to be adopted. And that is equal to *anuttara*, the state of *anuttara*, Lord Śiva.

---

39. Lit., the supreme, the unparalleled, an appelation of Lord Śiva.

Wisdom Verses 7 (47:46)

संसारजीर्णतरुमूलकलापकल्प-
संकल्पसान्तरतया परमार्थवह्नेः ।
स्युर्विस्फलिंगकणिका अपि चेत्तदन्ते
देदीप्यते विमलबोधहुताशराशिः ॥८३॥

saṁsārajīrṇatarumūlakalāpakalpa-
saṁkalpasāntaratayā paramārthavahneḥ /
syurvisphaliṅgakaṇikā api cettadante
dedīpyate vimalabodhahutāśarāśiḥ //83//

Here [Abhinavagupta] says: *saṁsāra jīrṇa tarumūla kalāpa kalpa saṁkalpa sāntaratayā paramārtha vahneḥ*, actually, this *saṁsāra*,...*

The wheel of repeated births and deaths is *saṁsāra*. Life succeeds , death succeeds life. Day succeeds night, night succeeds day. A month succeeds six months, six months succeeds a year. A year succeeds twelve years, and twelve years succeeds sixty years, and it goes on like that. This is the way of *saṁsāra*.

*...and actually *saṁsāra* is *jīrṇa taru*. *Jīrṅa taru* means, [*saṁsāra*] becomes *jīrṇa taru*. *Jīrṇa taru* means, a very old trunk you'll find of *saṁsāra*, it becomes older and older day-by-day by constant meditation. When you adopt meditation repeatedly every morning, each morning, each morning, *saṁsāra*, which is a big trunk of this tree of *saṁsāra*, it becomes, its roots become, torn. It is likely to fall down now at any moment. At any moment it may fall down and get finished by the repeated meditation on it. *Saṁkalpa sāntaratayā*, *saṁsāra jīrṇa tarumūla*, [*saṁsāra* is] *jīrṇa taru*, and at the root of that *saṁsāra*, at the root of that trunk, if at the root of the trunk only some particles of these...what are these called? It's called *tamiri*.

DENISE: On the roots?

SWAMIJI: On the roots. On the root of *saṁsāra*. When these particles of those...

INDERJI: Sparks.

SWAMIJI: Sparks, sparks, sparks of God consciousness, if sparks of God consciousness fall on the root of that *saṁsāra*...what is the root? The root is *saṁkalpa*, various thoughts, various engagements in this world. Those engagements produce roots of that trunk. And on those roots, if the constant falling of those sparks of meditation falls on those roots, *paramārtha vahneḥ*, of the sparks of *paramārtha* (*paramārtha vahneḥ*, the fire of God consciousness; the fire of God consciousness produces sparks and those sparks fall on the roots of that *saṁsāra*), if it is so, *syurvisphuliṅga kaṇikā api cet*, if only the sparks are there, it doesn't matter, *ante*, at the time of death or at the ending point of that *saṁsāra*, *dedīpyate*, finally shines *vimala bodha hutā śarāśiḥ*, the heaps of the light of God consciousness rises and this whole trunk is burnt to ashes. There is no meaning of *saṁsāra* again to exist anymore for him.

JOHN: At death. It happens for him at death?

SWAMIJI: Huh?

JOHN: At death it happens?

SWAMIJI: No, in the end, in the end when it is ripe, quite ripe. When sparks are there gathering, gathering, gathering, then a great fire is produced and it takes no time to burn to ashes this whole cycle of repeated births and deaths, and one becomes liberated for good. So you should go on putting sparks on it, of meditation. Don't think that it does not work. It works, it is going on, in time it will produce its fruit.

Now, it is threatening for those people who do not think of God each day and each morning.

Wisdom Verses 7 (55:11)

शास्त्रविरुद्धाचरणात्कृष्णं ये कर्म विदधते ।
तत्र भीमैर्लोकपुरुषैः पीड्यन्ते भोगपर्यन्तम् ॥८४॥

śāstraviruddhācaraṇātkṛṣṇaṁ ye karma vidadhate /
tatra bhīmairlokapuruṣaiḥ pīḍyante bhogaparyantam //84//
(not recited in full)

This is consolation for those…for instance, you are John, you have done so many mischievous things in youth, you have committed blunders–that is a fact, you know that–but once you have entered on the path of Śaivism, what will happen to those actions? Those actions you will have to suffer, undertake the sufferings of that fruit of those bad actions which you committed in your youth before entering in this Śaivite path. For that he puts some consolation for those.

Śāstra viruddhācaraṇāt kṛṣṇaṁ ye karma vidadhate, śāstra viruddhācaraṇāt, those who are acting against the directions of the *śāstra*s (scriptures), those who act in their lifetime against the directions of *śāstra*s, *kṛṣṇaṁ ye karma vidadhate*, those who do the actions of *kṛṣṇaṁ* (sinful actions), *vidadhate*, they who act like that,…

JOHN: Black actions, huh?

SWAMIJI: Black actions.[40]

…*tatra*, when they die, *bhīmairloka puruṣaiḥ*, fearful, those masses of servants, the slaves of the lord of death, those with fearful appearances, they come and, after death, they do–what they do?–*bhīmairloka puruṣaiḥ pīḍyante*, they squeeze them, they put them to task, they beat them–those people who act sinful acts in their lifetime. *Bhoga paryantam*, if they die by those beatings, thorough beatings, or by pricks of swords (laughs), they are likely to get another life at once for more pricks, and they cry there. They have to come across that punishment.

JOHN: So either they get tortured in hell…

SWAMIJI: Yes.

JOHN: Either they go to hell or if they die by a sword or something, then they get reborn quickly, and other things can happen.

SWAMIJI: Yes (laughs), and other punishment is likely to be done to them. But on the contrary:

Wisdom Verses 7 (58:48)

ये सकृदपि परमेशं शिवमेकाग्रेण चेतसा शरणं
यान्ति न ते नरकजुषः कृष्णं तेषां सुखाल्पतादायि ॥८५॥

---

40. *Kṛṣṇa* literally means "black".

ye sakṛdapi parameśaṁ śivamekāgreṇa cetasā śaraṇaṁ /
yānti na te narakajuṣaḥ kṛṣṇaṁ teṣāṁ sukhālpatādāyi //85//

On the contrary, those persons, *sakṛt api*, those who just, *parameśaṁ*, at the feet of Lord Śiva, *ekāgreṇa cetasā*, in a one-pointed way they take refuge of Lord Śiva's feet–those people, after committing so many mischievous things in their lifetime, the past period of lifetime–but if they at once take the refuge of Lord Śiva's feet with complete devotion, *yānti na te narakajuṣaḥ*, they don't experience the tragedy of hell, they don't experience the tragedy of hell anymore. But what will happen to those actions which they have done before that in their past period of youth? *Kṛṣṇaṁ*, their black actions (black actions means sinful actions), sinful actions, they will bear fruit, but what fruit [will] they bear for *him*, for that person who has taken refuge of Lord Śiva for good afterwards? After repenting and thinking, "I have done all these bad actions in my life; O Lord, save me, save me in the future," and takes refuge wholeheartedly,...

COOK: (Hindi) Do you want potato?

SWAMIJI: (Hindi) No potato today.

...*kṛṣṇaṁ teṣāṁ sukhālpatādāyi*, and when [their] turn comes of [receiving] the fruit of those actions which they have done in youth, that [fruit of their] sinful actions is for them–they don't get entry in hell, they are not pushed in hell for that–for that, only this happens to them that this joy of God consciousness becomes less for some period. The joy of God consciousness is lessened for some period. This is the fruit of those actions, not going to hell and getting beaten by those weapons. They don't get a beating afterwards if they once take refuge of Lord Śiva. This is the greatness of taking refuge of Lord Śiva.

Do you understand what...?

JOHN: So something happens.

SWAMIJI: What something?

JOHN: Some lessening. That's something.

SWAMIJI: Some lessening of joy, not a beating. They are not beaten blue (laughs). So it is worthwhile to take refuge of Lord Śiva, and it is never late. Whatever you have done in the past, nevermind, ignore it, take refuge of Lord Śiva and you'll remain fine. This is the *śloka* of the *Tantrāloka* in the eighth *āhnika*.

JOHN: This one we just [did].
SWAMIJI: Yes.

śāstraviruddhācaraṇātkṛṣṇaṁ ye karma vidadhate /
tatra bhīmairlokapuruṣaiḥ pīḍyante bhogaparyantam //84//
ye sakṛdapi parameśaṁ śivamekāgreṇa cetasā śaraṇaṁ /
yānti na te narakajuṣaḥ kṛṣṇaṁ teṣāṁ sukhālpatādāyi //85//
(verses repeated, not recited in full)

Yānti na te narakajuṣaḥ, they don't go to hell. *Kṛṣṇaṁ teṣāṁ sukhālpatādāyi*, the fruit of their black actions is only that the joy of God consciousness is lessened for sometime for them. It is a bit less, but joy is still knocking in the background. Joy! No pain, no beating (laughs). So it is good. So it is worthwhile to take refuge of Lord Śiva at any moment! It is never late!

Wisdom Verses 7 (1:04:31)

Vastutaḥ Śivasyaiva Sarvabhāvena Kartṛtvam
Everything is Done by Lord Śiva

अस्वतन्त्रस्य कर्तृत्वं नहि जातूपपद्यते ।
वस्तुतः सर्वभावानां कर्तेशानः परः शिवः ॥८६॥

asvatantrasya kartṛtvaṁ nahi jātūpapadyate /
vastutaḥ sarvabhāvānāṁ karteśānaḥ paraḥ śivaḥ //86//

Asvatantrasya, those who are not possessing *svātantrya* (independence), they cannot become doers. A potter cannot become the doer, the creator of a pot, the creator of those earthen pots. A potter cannot, it is not in the hands of a potter to make pots. It is not in the hands of a seed to get it sprout up because there is no *svātantrya* in a seed. How can it give a sprout to some plant? If a seed is kept in the earth, it produces a sprout, but it is not in the power of the seed that it produces a sprout, it is in His power that a sprout is produced by a seed. *Asvatantrasya*, it is *asvatantra*, he is dependent, a seed is dependent to His will. If there is His will, then it will produce a sprout from a seed, otherwise never. *Vastutaḥ*, in fact, *sarvabhāvānāṁ karteśānaḥ paraḥ śivaḥ*, whatever is done, whatever is produced, it is produced by Lord Śiva, not any other agency. If there are agencies, for instance, there is the agency of earth, there is the agency of seeds, there is the agency of water, the soaking of water, and it will produce [a sprout], but with all that, it will not produce any sprout until there is the hand of Lord Śiva there. In the same way, in a potter's hands, nothing is in a potter's hands. He cannot produce those pots unless there is the hand of Lord Śiva there. So, in fact, *sarva bhāvānāṁ kartā*, the doer of everything, whatever is this *kārin* and *kāri* (cause and effect), the theory of cause and effect takes place by Lord Śiva's will. There are no other aspects who have got the power to produce these effects from the cause. For instance, you are a woman. By mating with some man, you will produce a child. You won't produce a child and that man won't produce a child. It is the will of God that produces a child. So man and woman are not the cause and effect. Cause and effect, the theory of cause and effect is just nonsense, it is just for the time-being. It is adjusted, it is not real.

DENISE: It only appears to be that way.

SWAMIJI: Yes.

Wisdom Verses 7 (1:08:35)

तथा च तेषां हेतूनां संयोजनवियोजने ।
नियते शिव एवैकः स्वतंत्रः कर्तृतामियात् ॥८७॥

tathā ca teṣāṁ hetunāṁ saṁyojanaviyojane /
niyate śiva evaikaḥ svatantraḥ kartṛtāmiyāt //87//

Tathā ca, we will clarify this theory of cause and effect here. *Teṣāṁ hetunāṁ*, those causes which are meant as causes,…*[41]

41. "Which are those classes of causes? *Nimitta kāraṇa* (instrumental cause), *upādāna kāraṇa* (material cause)." *Tantrāloka* 9.35 (LJA archive).

What is the cause of a pot? When you produce a pot, an earthen pot, what is the cause of that? The cause is earth, the collection of earth, with water, and mixing of the earth with water, and putting it on that wheel, that earthen piece, and then the potter's doing this spinning the wheel, and then molding that earth. This is not done, this is not the theory of cause and effect. The cause and effect theory is in the hands of God. It is just our imagination that the potter has created this.

*...*teṣāṁ hetunāṁ saṁyojana viyojane*, cause and effect, *saṁyojana viyojane*, He will take you in such a way that you will meet what you are going to have, what you have longed for from hundreds of years. From hundreds of years you have been longing for some thing to act, and it has come true afterwards. And this cause and effect... for instance, you were longing to see me for all these three years, four years, and that was in His hands. So it has come true in the end. So the theory of cause and effect lies in the hands of God, not in the hands of human beings. *Saṁyojana*, if he is *saṁyojana*, mixing those [causes and effects] with each other, or *viyojane*, separating those [causes and effects] from each other, for this is responsible the will of God, not the will of a human being.[42] So Śiva is the only real cause of everything that happens in this world.

Wisdom Verses 7 (1:11:50)

बहवो गुरवः सन्ति शिष्यवित्तापहारकाः ।
दुर्लभोऽयं गुरुर्देवि शिष्यसन्तापहारकः ॥८८॥

bahavo guravaḥ santi śiṣyavittāpahārakāḥ /
durlabho'yaṁ gururdevi śiṣyasantāpahārakaḥ //88//
(not recited in full)

42. "He is the only cause [because] He unites, he handles, these so-called causes. *Saṁyojana-viyojane*, He has united a seed with a sprout, and a seed has become the cause of a sprout. He has not united that mountain with a sprout, so a mountain has not become the cause [of a sprout]." Ibid.

It is the best *śloka*. This I remember when I remember these so-called masters who snatch away all the jewelry, all money, all everything, all possessions from disciples and fill their bank balances–those masters, so-called masters.

Bahavo guravaḥ santi, there are such great, many masters seen in this world who *śiṣya vittāpahārakāḥ*, who are *apahārakāḥ*, who snatch away, *śiṣya vitta* (*śiṣya vitta* means, the money from their disciples), who snatch away, extract all the money from disciples. Such masters are available everywhere in this world. *Durlabho'yaṁ gururdevi*, O Pārvatī, that master is very rarely found, *śiṣya santāpahārakaḥ*, who is bent upon removing the pain and torture from the mind of his disciples, who removes only that pain. He has nothing to do with the money of his disciples. These kind of masters are rarely found in this world. Those masters who extract money from disciples are seen everywhere, in each and every corner of this [world].

Wisdom Verses 7 (1:13:53)

श्रीमत्सदाशिवपदेऽपि महोग्रकाली
भीमोत्कटभ्रुकुटिरेष्यति भङ्गभूमिः ।
इत्याकलय्य परमां स्थितिमेत्य काल-
सङ्कर्षिणीं भगवतीं हठतोऽधितिष्ठेत् ॥८९॥

śrīmatsadāśivapade'pi mahograkālī
bhīmotkaṭabhrukuṭireṣyati bhaṅgabhūmiḥ /
ityākalayya paramāṁ sthitimetya kāla-
saṅkarṣiṇīṁ bhagavatīṁ haṭhato'dhitiṣṭhet //89//
(verse from the Amṛteśvara Pūja)

SWAMIJI: *Śrīmat sadāśiva pade*, in Sadāśiva *pada*, in the kingdom of Sadāśiva also, when Kālī, Mahākālī (Mahākālī is the better-half of Lord Śiva), *mahograkālī*, when She raises Her eyelashes and squeezes Her eyelashes in a furious manner like this (Swamiji demonstrates), when She is full of wrath,...*

JOHN: Show. How?

SWAMIJI: (laughs) That is *bhīma utkaṭa bhrukuṭir. Bhīma* means, fearful; *utkaṭa* means, raised; *bhrukuṭi* means, eyelash. She raises [Her] eyelashes in such a way that it becomes *utkaṭa*; *utkaṭa* means, fearful, like this (Swamiji gives a fierce facial expression). "See, what are you doing? You silly girl!" Like this.

*...in the kingdom of Sadāśiva also, when this Kālī, *bhīma utkaṭa bhrukuṭir*, raises Her eyelashes in that fearful manner–that is like this (Swamiji demonstrates)–*eṣyati bhaṅga bhūmiḥ*, Sadāśiva along with his kingdom is shattered to pieces at once, in half a second. It takes less than half a second to get Sadāśiva his end along with his kingdom, he is no more existing at all. *Ityā kalayya*, this way, after considering this position of Mahākālī, that the kingdom of Sadāśiva also is shattered to pieces, nothingness, *paramāṁ sthitiṁ etya*, you should act in such a way that *paramāṁ sthitiṁ etya*, you should achieve the real existence of God consciousness with your body and soul wholeheartedly. And *kāla saṅkarṣinīṁ bhagavatiṁ*, that *bhagavatī* (goddess) who is Kālasaṅkarṣinī, who is fearful to the lord of death also, who can end the life of the lord of death also, that fearful Kālī, you should take refuge of fearful Kālī whatever happens to you (*haṭhatā*). Don't think of any other way, *bas*, just take the refuge of Mahākālī at once. Hold Her feet on your chest with great devotion. Don't think any other thing at all. She may kill you or She may have you or She may protect you, take refuge in Her.

JOHN: So this is that Mahākālī who has the power to destroy Sadāśiva in one second.

SWAMIJI: In one second with this, *bas*, he has nothing to do.

JOHN: Just with a furious glance.

SWAMIJI: A furious glance, *pza-pza-pza*, *bas*, he is no more existing, finished!

JOHN: So then, a devotee should take, seek refuge in Her immediately?

SWAMIJI: *Haṭhata*, whatever may happen. If She beats him, it doesn't matter. After all, She is Mother, She won't beat to that extent (laughs). You must, *bas*, let Her beat you, beat your back wholeheartedly, but don't leave Her feet separated.

JOHN: You said, "Put Her feet on your chest," means that She walks on you like that?

SWAMIJI: Yes.

JOHN: Like on those pictures or those *murtis* (forms) She is standing on…?

SWAMIJI: Yes. *Bas*, it is finished.

JOHN: So Saṅkarṣinī Kālī is…?

SWAMIJI: Saṅkarṣinīṁ, Kālasaṅkarṣinīṁ Kalī. "*Kāla*" is in the third line. Ending [of the] third line is "*kāla*". Kālasaṅkarṣinīṁ, who kills the lord of *kāla* (time), who kills Mahākāla. That Kālī kills Mahākāla.

JOHN: Kills Mahākāla means, the lord of death.

SWAMIJI: The lord of death. The lord of death is shattered to pieces by Her one glance. When the lord of death is also killed, what remains fearful then afterwards? Fearful was the lord of death, [but] the lord of death has taken its end there. So Kālasaṁkarṣinī *bhagavatī* is Mother, really the Mother, protecting everybody. You should take refuge at any cost. Take Her refuge and everything will be fine.

JOHN: *Saṅkarṣinī* means, beautiful?

SWAMIJI: No. *Saṅkarṣinī*, who puts Mahākāla to his end.

JOHN: This is that same Saṅkarṣinī Kālī that we talk about in the next verse:

tanmadhye tu parādevī dakṣine ca parāparā /
aparā vāmaśṛṅge tu madhyasṛṅgo'rdhvatah śṛṇu //
yā sā saṁkarṣinī kālī parātītā vyavasthitā /

SWAMIJI: Yes.

JOHN: That's the same.

SWAMIJI: Yes, it is this. There is *triśula* (trident) in triple…*triśula* you know already.

JOHN: Yes.

SWAMIJI: It has got three…

DENISE: Prongs?

SWAMIJI:…three forks. One is on the right side, another is on the left side, and the central one is in the center (this is the third one). That is *tanmadhye tu parādevī*, in the center is the residence of *parādevī*, *parāśakti. Dakṣine ca parāparā*, *parāparā* is on the right side of that fork of the *triśula. Aparā vāmaśṛṅge tu*, *aparā śakti* is on the left fork. In the central fork is *parā*, on the right fork is…

JOHN: *Dakṣine, parāparā.*

SWAMIJI:...*parāparā*, and *aparā* is on the left side. *Tanmadhye tu parādevī dakṣine ca parāparā*, on the right side is *parāparā*, *aparā vāmaśṛṅge tu*, on the left side is *aparā*, *madhyasṛṅgo'rdhvatah śṛṇu*, and this *madhya sṛṅga* (middle point), on the top of that *sṛṅga* (point), I will tell you what is existing there–on the top.

DENISE: Saṅkarṣinī Kālī?

JOHN: On the top means more than the center?

SWAMIJI: Above the center.

DENISE: Saṅkarṣinī Kālī?

SWAMIJI: *Yā sā saṁkarṣinī kālī parātītā*, there is Kālasaṅkarṣinī Kālī on the top-center, where Lord Śiva lies dead on that top-center, and She dances over it, over that dead body.

JOHN: So He is dead. Why is He dead, lying dead? "Dead" means?

SWAMIJI: With peace. He does not move at all because He enjoys the blissful touch of Her feet, the feet of that Kālasaṅkarṣinī Kālī, who has cornered the lord of death for good.

JOHN: Finished him.

SWAMIJI: Kālasaṅkarṣinī is that [Goddess] who has cornered the lord of death.

Wisdom Verses 7 (1:24:32) end

Appendix

Wisdom of Kashmir Shaivism
(verses only for recitation)

अस्तङ्गतवति प्राणे त्वपानेऽभ्युदयोन्मुखे ।
तावत्सा कुम्भकावस्था योगिभिरानुभूयते ॥ १ ॥

astaṅgatavati prāṇe tvapāne'bhyudayonmukhe /
tāvatsā kumbhakāvāsthā yogibhirānubhūyate //1//

यथा निमीलने काले प्रपञ्चो नैव दृश्यते ।
तथैवोन्मीलने स्याच्चेदेतद्ध्यानस्य लक्षणम् ॥ २ ॥

yathā nimīlane kāle prapañco naiva dṛśyate /
tathaivonmīlane syāccedetatdhyānasya lakṣaṇam //2//

प्रकाशमाने परमार्थभानौ नश्यत्यविद्यातिमिरे समस्ते ।
तदा बुधाः निर्मलदृष्टयोऽपि किञ्चिन्न पश्यन्ति भवप्रपञ्चम्
॥ ३ ॥

prakāśamāne paramārthabhānau naśyatyavidyātimire samaste /
tadā budhā nirmaladṛṣtayo'pi kiñcinna paśyanti bhavaprapañcam //3//

प्रनष्टवायुसञ्चारः पाषाण इव निश्चलः ।
परजीवैक्यधर्मज्ञो योगी योगविदुच्यते ॥४॥

pranaṣṭavāyusañcāraḥ pāṣāṇa iva niścalaḥ /
parajīvaikyadharmajñyo yogī yoga viducyate //4//

ब्रह्मविष्णुमहेशादिदेवता भूतजातयः ।
नाशमेवानुधावन्ति तस्माच्छ्रेयः समभ्यसेत् ॥५॥

brahma viṣṇumaheśādi devatā bhūtajātayaḥ /
nāśamevānudhāvanti tasmācchreyaḥ samabhyaset //5//

अज्ञो जन्तुरनीशोऽयमात्मनः सुखदुःखयोः ।
ईश्वरप्रेरितो गच्छेत् श्वभ्रं वा स्वर्गमेव वा ॥६॥

ajño janturanīśo'yamātmanaḥ sukhaduḥkhayoḥ /
īśvaraprerito gacchet śvabhraṁ vā svargameva vā //6//

यावन्नैव प्रविशति चरन्मरु तो मध्यमार्गे ।
यावद्बिन्दुर्न भवति दृढं प्राणवातप्रबन्धात् ॥७॥
यावन्नैव सहजसदृशं जायते चैव तत्त्वं ।
तावत्सर्वं तदिदमखिलं दम्भमिथ्याप्रलापम् ॥८॥

yāvannaiva praviśati caran maruto madhyamārge /
yāvat bindur na bhavati dṛḍhaṁ prāṇavāta prabandhāt //7//

yāvannaiva sahajasadṛśaṁ jāyate caiva tattvaṁ /
tāvat sarvaṁ tadidamakhilaṁ dambhamithyāpralāpam //8//

आश्यानं चिद्रसस्यौघं साकारत्वमुपागतम् ।
जगद्रूपतया वन्दे प्रत्यक्षं भैरवं वपुः ॥ ९ ॥

āśyānaṁ cidrasasyaughaṁ sākāratvamupāgatam /
jagadrūpatayā vande pratyakṣaṁ bhairavaṁ vapuḥ //9//

उज्झित्वात्मसमाधानं ये ध्यायन्त्यन्यदेवताः ।
भिक्ष्यन्ते भूरिवित्तास्ते भिक्षित्वापि बुभुक्षिताः ॥ १० ॥

ujjhitvātma samādhānaṁ ye dhyāyantyanyadevatāḥ /
bhikṣyante bhūrivittāste bhikṣitvāpi bubhukṣitāḥ //10//

जाग्रत्स्वप्नसुषुप्तान्यत्तदतीतानि यान्यपि ।
तान्यप्यमुष्यनाथस्य स्वातन्त्र्यलहरीभरः ॥ ११ ॥

jāgrat svapnasuṣuptānyattadatītāni yānyapi /
tānyapyamuṣyanāthasya svātantryalaharībharaḥ //11//

महामन्त्रेशमन्त्रेशमन्त्राः शिवपुरोगमाः ।
अकलौ सकलश्चेति शिवस्यैव विभूतयः ॥ १२ ॥

mahāmantreśamantreśa mantrāḥ śivapurogamāḥ /
akalau sakalaśceti śivasyaiva vibhūtayaḥ //12//

सृष्टिस्थितितिरोधान संहारानुग्रहादि च ।
तुर्यमित्यपि देवस्य बहुशक्तित्वजृम्भितम् ॥ १३ ॥

sṛṣṭisthititirodhāna saṁhārānugrahādi ca /
turyamityapi devasya bahuśaktitvajṛmbhitam //13//

तस्य शक्तय एवैतास्तिस्रो भान्ति परादिकाः ।
सृष्टौ स्थितौ लये तुर्ये तेनैताः द्वादशोदिताः ॥ १४ ॥

tasya śaktaya evaitāstisro bhānti parādikāḥ /
sṛṣṭau sthitau laye turye tenaitāḥ dvādaśoditāḥ //14//

बहुशक्तित्वमस्योक्तं शिवस्य यदतो महान् ।
कलातत्त्वपुरार्णाणुपदादिर्भेदविस्तरः ॥ १५ ॥

bahuśaktitvamasyoktaṁ śivasya yadato mahān /
kalātattvapurārṇāṇupadādirbhedavistaraḥ //15//

कदाचिद्भक्तियोगेन कर्मणा विद्ययापि वा ।
ज्ञानधर्मोपदेशेन मन्त्रैर्वा दीक्षयापि वा ॥ १६ ॥
एवमाद्यैरनेकैश्च प्रकारैः परमेश्वरः ।
संसारिणोऽनुगृह्णाति विश्वस्य जगतः पतिः ॥ १७ ॥
(युगलकं)

kadācidbhaktiyogena karmaṇā vidyayāpi vā /
jñānadharmopadeśena mantrairvā dīkṣayāpi vā //16//
evamādyairanekaiśca prakāraiḥ parameśvaraḥ /
saṁsāriṇo'nugṛhṇāti viśvasya jagataḥ patiḥ //17//

क्रमाभावान्न युगपत्तदभावात्क्रमोऽपि न ।
क्रमाक्रमकथातीतं संवित्तत्त्वं सुनिर्मलम् ॥१८॥

kramābhāvānna yugapattadabhāvātkramo'pi na /
kramākramakathātītaṁ saṁvittattvaṁ sunirmalam //18//

अदीक्षितानां पुरतो नोच्चरेत् शिवसंहिताम् ।
तमाराध्य ततस्तुष्टाद्दीक्षामासाध्य शांकरीम् ॥१९॥
येन केनाप्युपायेन गुरुमाराध्य भक्तितः ।
तद्दीक्षाक्रमयोगेन शास्त्रार्थं वेत्त्यसौ ततः ॥२०॥
अभिषेकं समासाध्य यो भवेत् स तु कल्पितः ।
सन्नप्यशेषापाशौघविनिवर्तनकोविदः ॥२१॥
(तिलकं)

adīkṣitānāṁ purato noccaret śivasaṁhitām /
tamārādhya tatastuṣṭāddīkṣāmāsādhya śāṁkarīṁ //19//
yena kenāpyupāyena gurumārādhya bhaktitaḥ /
taddīkṣākramayogena śāstrārthaṁ vettyasau tataḥ //20//
abhiṣekaṁ samāsādhya yo bhavet sa tu kalpitaḥ /
sannapyaśeṣāpāśaughavinivartanakovidaḥ //21//

संसारमोहनाशाय शब्दबोधो नहि क्षमः ।
न निवर्तेत तिमिरं कदाचिद्दीपवर्तया ॥२२॥

saṁsāramohanāśāya śabdabodho nahi kṣamaḥ /
na nivarteta timiraṁ kadāciddīpavartayā //22//

अभ्यस्य वेदशास्त्राणि सारं ज्ञात्वाथबुद्धिमान् ।
पलालमिव धान्यार्थे त्यजेच्छास्त्रमशेषतः ॥२३॥

abhyasya vedaśāstrāṇi sāraṁ jñātvātha buddhimān /
palālamiva dhānyārthe tyajecchāstramaśeṣataḥ //23//

षट्दर्शनमहाकूपे पतिताः पशवः प्रिये ।
न जानन्ति परं तत्त्वं दर्वी पाकरसं यथा ॥२४॥

ṣaṭ darśanamahākūpe patitāḥ paśavaḥ priye /
na jānanti paraṁ tattvaṁ darvī pākarasaṁ yathā //24//

यदा तु वैचित्र्यवशाज्जानीयात्तस्य तादृशम् ।
विपरीतप्तवृतित्त्वं ज्ञानं तस्मादुपाहरेत् ॥२५॥

yadā tu vaicitryavaśājjānīyāttasya tādṛśam /
viparītaptavṛtittvaṁ jñānaṁ tasmādupāharet //25//

तं च त्यजेत्पापवृत्तिं भवेत्तु ज्ञानतत्परः ॥२५-१/२॥

taṁ ca tyajetpāpavṛttiṁ bhavettu jñānatatparaḥ //25b//

यदा किञ्चिज्ज्ञोऽहं द्विप इव मदान्धः समभवम् ।
तदा सर्वज्ञोऽस्मीत्यभवदवलिप्तं मम मनः ॥२६॥
यदा किञ्चित् किञ्चिद् बुधजनसकाशादवगतम् ।
तदा मूर्खोऽस्मीति ज्वर इवमदो मे व्यपगतः ॥२७॥

yadā kiñcijjño'haṁ dvipa iva madāndhaḥ samabhavam /
tadā sarvajño'smītyabhavadavaliptaṁ mama manaḥ //26//
yadā kiñcitkiñcidbudhajanasakāśādavagatam /
tadā mūrkho'smīti jvara ivamado me vyapagataḥ //27//

शासनरोधनपालनपाचनयोगात्स सर्वमुपकुरुते ।
तेन पतिः श्रेयोमय एव शिवो नाशिवं किमपि तत्र ॥२८॥

śāsanarodhanapālanapācanayogātsa sarvamupakurute /
tena patiḥ śreyomaya eva śivo nāśivaṁ kimapi tatra //28//

ईदृग्रूपं कियदपि रुद्रोपेन्द्रादिषु स्फुरेद्येनः ।
तेनावच्छेदनुदे परममहत्पदविशेषणमुपातम् ॥२९॥

īdṛgrūpaṁ kiyadapi rudropendrādiṣu sphuredyenaḥ /
tenāvacchedanude paramamahatpadaviśeṣaṇamupātam //29//

देवो ह्यन्वर्थशास्त्रोक्तैः शब्दैः समुपदिश्यते ।
महाभैरवदेवोऽयं पतिर्यः परमः शिवः ॥ ३० ॥

devo hyanvarthaśāstroktaiḥ śabdaiḥ samupadiśyate /
mahābhairavadevo'yaṁ patiryaḥ paramaḥ śivaḥ //30//

विश्वं बिभर्ति पूरणधारणयोगेन तेन च भ्रियते ॥ ३१ ॥
भैरव इति गुरुभिरिमैरन्वर्थैः संस्तुतः शास्त्रे ॥
सविमर्शतया रवरूपतश्च संसार भीरुहितकृच्च ॥ ३२ ॥
भैरव इति गुरुभिरिमैरन्वर्थैः संस्तुतः शास्त्रे ॥

viśvaṁ bibharti pūraṇadhāraṇayogena tena ca bhriyate //31//
bhairava iti gurubhirimair anvarthaiḥ saṁstutaḥ śāstre /
savimarśatayā ravarūpataśca saṁsāra bhīruhitakṛcca //32//
bhairava iti gurubhirimair anvarthaiḥ saṁstutaḥ śāstre /

संसारभीतिजनिताद्रवात्परामर्शतोऽपि हृदि जातः ॥ ३३ ॥
भैरव इति गुरुभिरिमैरन्वर्थैः संस्तुतः शास्त्रे ॥
प्रकटीभूतं भवभयविमर्शनं शक्तिपाततो येन ॥ ३४ ॥
भैरव इति गुरुभिरिमैरन्वर्थैः संस्तुतः शास्त्रे ॥

saṁsārabhītijanitādravātparāmarśato'pi hṛdi jātaḥ //33//
bhairava iti gurubhirimair anvarthaiḥ saṁstutaḥ śāstre /
prakaṭībhūtaṁ bhavabhayavimarśanaṁ śaktipātato yena //34//
bhairava iti gurubhirimair anvarthaiḥ saṁstutaḥ śāstre /

नक्षत्रप्रेरककालतत्त्वसंशोषकारिणो ये च ।
कालग्रासससमाधानरसिकमनःसु तेषु च प्रकटः ॥ ३५ ॥

nakṣatraprerakakālatattvasaṁśoṣakāriṇo ye ca /
kālagrāsasamādhānarasikamanaḥsu teṣu ca prakaṭaḥ //35//

सङ्कोचीपशुजनभिये यासां रवणं स्वकरणदेवीनाम् ।
अन्तर्बहिश्चतुर्विधखेचर्यादिकगणस्यापि ॥ ३६ ॥
तस्य स्वामी संसारवृत्तिविघट्टनमहाभीमः ।
भैरव इति गुरुभिरिमैरन्वर्थैः संस्तुतः शास्त्रे ॥ ३७ ॥
(कुलकं)

saṅkocipaśujanabhiye yāsāṁ ravaṇaṁ svakaraṇadevīnām /
antarbahiścaturvidhakhecaryādikagaṇasyāpi //36//
tasya svāmī saṁsāravṛttivighaṭṭanamahābhīmaḥ /
bhairava iti gurubhirimairanvarthaiḥ saṁstutaḥ śāstre //37//

विश्वैकरूपविश्वात्म विश्वसर्गादिकारणम् ।
परप्रकाशवपुषं स्तुमः स्वच्छन्दभैरवम् ॥ ३८ ॥

viśvaikarūpaviśvātma viśvasargādi kāraṇam /
paraprakāśavapuṣaṁ stumaḥ svacchandabhairavam //38//

मध्यप्राणनिविष्टहंसपरमः यो रोमकूपाश्रयः ।
प्राणः सूक्ष्मविमर्शशालिवपुषः सार्धत्रिकोटयात्मकः ॥ ३९ ॥
तान्मन्त्रात्मतया विलोमयति यः स्वच्छन्दनाथः परो ।
देवोऽसौ विदधातु भैरववपुः तेजः परं शाश्वतम् ॥ ४० ॥

madhyaprāṇaniviṣṭahaṁsa paramaḥ yo romakūpāśrayaḥ /
prāṇaḥ sūkṣmavimarśaśālivapuṣaḥ sārdhatrikoṭayātmakaḥ //39//
tānmantrātmatayā vilomayati yaḥ svacchandanāthaḥ paro /
devo'sau vidadhātu bhairavavapuḥ tejaḥ paraṁ śāśvatam //40//

दुष्करं सुकरीकर्तुं दुःखं सुखयितुं तथा ।
एकवीरा स्मृतिर्यस्य तं स्मरामः स्मरद्विषम् ॥ ४१ ॥

duṣkaraṁ sukarīkartuṁ duḥkhaṁ sukhayituṁ tathā /
ekavīrā smṛtiryasya taṁ smarāmaḥ smaradviṣam //41//

क्षमः कां नापदं हन्तुं कां दातुं संपदं न वा ।
योऽसौ सो दयितोऽस्माकं देवदेवो वृषध्वजः ॥ ४२ ॥

kṣamaḥ kāṁ nāpadaṁ hantuṁ kāṁ dātuṁ saṁpadaṁ na vā /
yo'sau so dayito'smākaṁ devadevo vṛṣadhvajaḥ //42//

दृष्ट्वा शिष्यं जराग्रस्तं व्याधिभिः परिपीडितम् ।
उत्क्रमय्य ततस्त्वेनं परतत्त्वे नियोजयेत् ॥ ४३ ॥

सर्वमप्यथवा भोगं मन्यमानो विरूपकम् ।
उत्क्रमय्य ततस्त्वेनं परतत्त्वे नियोजयेत् ॥ ४४ ॥

dṛṣṭvā śiṣyaṁ jarāgrastaṁ vyādhibhiḥ paripīḍitam /
utkramayya tatastvenaṁ paratattve niyojayet //43//
sarvamapyathavā bhogaṁ manyamāno virūpakam /
utkramayya tatastvenaṁ paratattve niyojayet //44//

तामाश्रित्योर्ध्वमार्गेण चन्द्रसूर्यावुभावपि ।
सौषुम्नेऽध्वन्यस्तमितो हित्वा ब्रह्माण्डगोचरम् ॥ ४५ ॥
तदा तस्मिन्महाव्योम्नि प्रलीनशशिभास्करे ।
सौषुप्तपदवन्मूढः प्रबुद्धः स्यादनावृतः ॥ ४६ ॥
(निलकं)

tāmāśrityordhvamārgeṇa candrasūryāvubhāvapi /
sauṣumne'dhvanyastamito hitvā brahmāṇḍagocaram //45//
tadā tasminmahāvyomni pralīnaśaśibhāskare /
sauṣuptapadavanmūḍhaḥ prabuddhaḥ syādanāvṛtaḥ //46//

यामवस्थां समालम्ब्य यदयं मम वक्ष्यति ।
तदवश्यं करिष्येऽहमिति संकल्प्य तिष्ठति ॥ ४७ ॥

yāmavasthāṁ samālambya yadayaṁ mama vakṣyati /
tadavaśyaṁ kariṣye'hamiti saṁkalpya tiṣṭhati //47//

यत्रोपरमते चित्तं निरुद्धं योगसेवनात् ।
यत्र चैवात्मनात्मानं पश्यन्नात्मनि तुष्यति ॥४८॥
सुखमात्यन्तिकं यत्तद्बुद्धिग्राह्यमतीन्द्रियम् ।
वेत्ति यत्र न चैवायं स्थितश्चलति तत्त्वतः ॥४९॥
यं लब्ध्वा चापरं लाभं मन्यते नाधिकं ततः ।
यस्मिन् स्थितो न दुःखेन गुरुणापि विचाल्यते ॥५०॥
तं विद्याद्दुःखसंयोगवियोगं योगसंज्ञितम् ।
स निश्चयेन योक्तव्यो योगोऽनिर्वण्णचेतसा ॥५१॥

yatroparamate cittaṁ niruddhaṁ yogasevanāt /
yatra caivātmanātmānaṁ paśyannātmani tuṣyati //48//
sukhamātyantikaṁ yattadbuddhigrāhyamatīndriyam /
vetti yatra na caivāyaṁ sthitaścalati tattvataḥ //49//
yaṁ labdhvā cāparaṁ lābhaṁ manyate nādhikaṁ tataḥ /
yasmin sthito na duḥkhena guruṇāpi vicālyate //50//
taṁ vidyādduḥkhasaṁyogaviyogaṁ yogasaṁjñitam /
sa niścayena yoktavyo yogo'nirviṇṇacetasā //51//

प्रशान्तमनसं ह्येनं योगिनं सुखमुत्तमम् ।
उपैति शान्तरजसं ब्रह्मभूतमकल्मषम् ॥५२॥

praśāntamanasaṁ hyenaṁ yoginaṁ sukhamuttamam /
upaiti śāntarajasaṁ brahmabhūtamakalmaṣam //52//

युञ्जन्नेवं सदात्मानं योगी नियतमानसः ।
सुखेन ब्रह्मसंयोगमत्यन्तमधिगच्छति ॥५३॥
(कुलकं)

yuñjannevaṁ sadātmānaṁ yogī niyatamānasaḥ /
sukhena brahmasaṁyogamatyantamadhigacchati //53//

विघ्नायुतसहस्रं तु परोत्साहसमन्वितम् ।
प्रहरत्यनिशं जन्तोः सद्वस्त्वभिमुखस्य च ।
विशेषतो भवाम्बोधिसमुत्तरणकारिणः ॥५४॥

vighnāyutasahasraṁ tu parotsāhasamanvitam /
praharatyaniśaṁ jantoḥ sadvastvabhimukhasya ca /
viśeṣato bhavāmbodhisamuttaraṇakāriṇaḥ //54//

रामः किमुच्यते देव योऽत्रस्थः स च कः प्रभो ।
तस्याभ्यासः कथं नाम ब्रूहि मे परमेश्वर ॥५५॥

rāmaḥ kimucyate deva yo'trasthaḥ sa ca kaḥ prabho /
tasyābhyāsaḥ kathaṁ nāma brūhi me parameśvara //55//

गतिः स्थानं स्वप्नजाग्रदुन्मेषणनिमेषणे ।
धावनं प्लवनं चैव आयासः शक्तिवेदनम् ॥५६॥
बुद्धिभेदास्तथा भावाः संज्ञाः कर्माण्यनेकशः ।

एतच्चतुर्दशविधं रामं तु परिकीर्तितम् ॥५७॥
ऊर्ध्वं त्यक्त्वाधो विशेत् स रामस मध्यदेशगः ॥
(युगलकं)

gatiḥ sthānaṁ svapnajāgradunmeṣaṇanimeṣaṇe /
dhāvaṇaṁ plavanaṁ caiva āyāsaḥ śaktivedanam //56//
buddhibhedāstathā bhāvāḥ saṁjñāḥ karmāṇyanekaśaḥ /
etaccaturdaśavidhaṁ rāmaṁ tu parikīrtitam //57//

ऊर्ध्वं त्यक्त्वाधो विशेत् स रामस्थो मध्यदेशगः ॥५८॥

ūrdhvaṁ tyaktvādho viśet sa rāmastho madhyadeśagaḥ //58//

न मोक्षो नभसः पृष्टे न पाताले न भूतले ।
सर्वाशासंक्षये चेतः क्षयो मोक्ष इतीष्यते ॥५९॥
(इति वेदान्ते)

na mokṣo nabhasaḥ pṛṣṭe na pātāle na bhūtale /
sarvāśāsaṁkṣaye cetaḥ kṣayo mokṣa itīṣyate //59//

मोक्षस्य नैव किञ्चिद् धामास्ति न चापि गमनमन्यत्र ।
अज्ञानग्रन्थभिदा स्वशक्त्यभिव्यक्तता भोक्षः ॥६०॥

mokṣasya naiva kiñcid dhāmāsti na cāpi gamanamanyatra /
ajñānagranthabhidā svaśaktyabhivyaktatā mokṣaḥ //60//

मोक्षो हि नाम नैवान्यः स्वरूपप्रथनं हि सः ।
स्वरूपं चात्मनः संविन्नान्यत्तत्र तु याः पुनः ॥६१॥
क्रियादिकाः शक्तयस्ताः संविद्रूपाधिका नहि ।
असंविद्रूपतायोगाद्धर्मिणश्चानिरूपणात् ॥६२॥
(युगलकं)

mokṣo hi nāma naivānyaḥ svarūpaprathanaṁ hi saḥ /
svarūpaṁ cātmanaḥ saṁvinnānyattatra tu yāḥ punaḥ //61//
kriyādikāḥ śaktayastāḥ saṁvidrūpādhikā nahi /
asaṁvidrūpatāyogāddharmiṇaścānirūpaṇāt //62//

परमेश्वरशास्त्रे च न च काणाददृष्टिवत् ।
शक्तीनां धर्मरूपाणामाश्रयः कोऽपि कथ्यते ॥६३॥

parameśvaraśāstre ca na ca kāṇādadṛṣṭivat /
śaktīnāṁ dharmarūpāṇāmāśrayaḥ ko'pi kathyate //63//

एक एव मनोदेवो जितः सर्वार्थसिद्धिदः ।
उन्यश्च विफलः क्लेशः सर्वेषां तज्जयं विना ॥६४॥

eka eva manodevo jitaḥ sarvārthasiddhidaḥ /
unyaśca viphalaḥ kleśaḥ sarveṣāṁ tajjayaṁ vinā //64//

सोऽपि स्वातन्त्र्यधाम्ना चेदप्यनिर्मलसंविदाम् ।
अनुग्रहं चिकीर्षुस्तद्भाविनं विधिमाश्रयेत् ॥ ६५ ॥

so'pi svātantryadhāmnā cedapyanirmalasaṁvidām /
anugrahaṁ cikīrṣustadbhāvinaṁ vidhimāśrayet //65//

तदर्थमेव चास्यापि परमेश्वररूपिणः ।
तदभ्युपायशास्त्रादिश्रवणाध्ययनादरः ॥ ६६ ॥

tadarthameva cāsyāpi parameśvararūpiṇaḥ /
tadabhyupāyaśāstrādiśravaṇādhyayanādaraḥ //66//

नहि तस्य स्वतन्त्रस्य क्वापि कुत्रापि खण्डना ।
नानिर्मलचित्तः पुंसोऽनुग्रहस्त्वनुपायकः ॥ ६७ ॥
(कुलकं)

nahi tasya svatantraśya kvāpi kutrāpi khaṇḍanā /
nānirmalacittaḥ puṁso'nugrahastvanupāyakaḥ //67//

अयं रसो येन मनागवाप्तः स्वच्छन्दचेष्टानिरतस्य तस्य ।
समाधियोगव्रतमन्त्रमुद्रा जपादिचर्या विषवद्विभाति ॥ ६८ ॥

ayaṁ raso yena manāgavāptaḥ svacchandaceṣṭāniratasya tasya /
samādhiyogavratamantramudrā japādicaryā viṣavadvibhāti //68//

तत्त्वमात्मस्थमज्ञात्वा मूढःशास्त्रेषु मुह्यति ।
गोपः कुक्षिगतं छागं कूपे पश्यति दुर्मतिः ॥ ६९ ॥

tattvamātmasthamajñātvā mūḍhaḥ śāstreṣu muhyati /
gopaḥ kukṣigataṁ chāgaṁ kūpe paśyati durmatiḥ //69//

बहिर्मुखस्य मन्त्रस्य वृत्तयो या प्रकीर्तिताः ।
ता एवान्तर्मुखस्यास्य शक्तयः परिकीर्तिताः ॥ ७० ॥

bahirmukhasya mantrasya vṛttayo yā prakīrtitāḥ /
tā evāntarmukhasyāsya śaktayaḥ parikīrtitāḥ //70//

हस्तं हस्तेन संपीड्य दन्तैर्दन्तांश्च पीडयन् ।
अङ्गान्यंगैर्समाक्रम्य जयेदादौ स्वकं मनः ॥ ७१ ॥

hastaṁ hastena saṁpīḍya dantairdantāṁśca pīḍayan /
aṅgānyaṁgairsamākramya jayedādau svakaṁ manaḥ //71//

तं ये पश्यन्ति ताद्रूप्यक्रमेणामलसंविदः ।
तेऽपि तद्रूपिणस्तावत्येवास्यानुग्रहात्मता ॥ ७२ ॥

taṁ ye paśyanti tādrūpyakrameṇāmalasaṁvidaḥ /
te'pi tadrūpiṇastāvatyevāsyānugrahātmatā //72//

पूर्णानन्दस्वभावः स्वजनहितकृते माययोपात्तकायः ।
कारुण्यादुद्दिधीर्षुर्जनमनवरतं मोहपङ्के निमग्नम् ॥ ७३ ॥

pūrṇānandasvabhāvaḥ svajanahitakṛte māyayopāttakāyaḥ /
kāruṇyāduddidhīrṣurjanamanavaratam̐ mohapan̐ke nimagnam //73//

आविश्यान्तर्वसिष्ठं बहिरपि कलयन् शिष्यभावं वितेने ।
यः संवादेन शास्त्रामृत जलधिममुं रामचन्द्रं प्रपद्ये ॥ ७४ ॥

āviśyāntarvasiṣṭham̐ bahirapi kalayan śiṣyabhāvam̐ vitene /
yaḥ sam̐vādena śāstrāmṛta jaladhimamum̐ rāmacandram̐ prapadye //74//

गुरोर्वाक्याद्युक्तिप्रचयरचनोन्मार्जनवशात् ।
समाश्वासाच्छास्त्रं प्रतिसमुदिताद्वापि कथितात् ॥ ७५ ॥
विलीने शङ्काभ्रे हृदयगगनोद्भासिमहसः ।
प्रभोः सूर्यस्येव स्पृशत चरणान्ध्वान्तजयिनः ॥ ७६ ॥

gurorvākyādyuktipracayaracanonmārjanavaśāt /
samāśvāsācchāstram̐ pratisamuditādvāpi kathitāt //75//
vilīne śan̐kābhre hṛdayagaganodbhāsimahasaḥ /
prabhoḥ sūryasyeva spṛśata caraṇāndhvāntajayinaḥ //76//

प्रज्ञाप्रासादमारुह्य अशोच्यःशोचतो जनान् ।
भूमिष्ठानिव शैलस्थः सर्वान्प्राज्ञोऽनुपश्यति ॥ ७७ ॥

prajñāprāsādamāruhya aśocyaḥ śocato janān /
bhūmiṣṭhāniva śailasthaḥ sarvānprājño'nupaśyati //77//

अविकल्पपथारूढो येन येन पथा विशेत् ।
धरासदाशिवान्तेन तेन तेन शिवीभवेत् ॥ ७८ ॥

avikalpapathārūḍho yena yena pathā viśet /
dharāsadāśivāntena tena tena śivībhavet //78//

यथास्थितः तथैवास्व मा गाः बाह्यमथान्तरम् ।
केवलं चिद्विकासेन विकारनिकराञ्जहि ॥ ७९ ॥

yathāsthitaḥ tathaivāsva mā gāḥ bāhyamathāntaram /
kevalaṁ cidvikāsena vikāranikarāñjahi //79//

अर्थेषु तद्भोगविधौ तदुत्थे दुःखे सुखे वा गलिताभिशङ्कम् ।
अनाविशन्तोऽपि निमग्नचित्ताः जानन्ति वृत्तिक्षयसौख्य-
मन्तः ॥ ८० ॥

artheṣu tadbhogavidhau tadutthe duḥkhe sukhe vā galitābhiśaṅkam /
anāviśanto'pi nimagnacittāḥ jānanti vṛttikṣayasaukhyamantaḥ //80/

अनुत्तरेऽभ्युपायोऽत्र ताद्रूप्यादेव वर्णितः ।
ज्वलितेष्वपि दीपेषु घर्मांशुः किं न भासते ॥ ८१ ॥

anuttare'bhyupāyo'tra tādrūpyādeva varṅitaḥ /
jvaliteṣvapi dīpeṣu gharmāṁśuḥ kiṁ na bhāsate //81//

ततोऽपि परमं ज्ञानमुपायादिविवर्जितम् । a
आनन्दशक्तिविश्रान्तमनुत्तरमिहोच्यते ॥८२॥

tato'pi paramaṁ jñānamupāyādivivarjitam /
ānandaśaktiviśrāntamanuttaramihocyate //82//

संसारजीर्णतरुमूलकलापकल्प-
संकल्पसान्तरतया परमार्थवह्नेः ।
स्युर्विस्फलिंगकणिका अपि चेत्तदन्ते
देदीप्यते विमलबोधहुताशराशिः ॥८३॥

saṁsārajīrṇatarumūlakalāpakalpa-
saṁkalpasāntaratayā paramārthavahneḥ /
syurvisphaliṅgakaṇikā api cettadante
dedīpyate vimalabodhahutāśarāśiḥ //83//

शास्त्रविरुद्धाचरणात्कृष्णं ये कर्म विदधते ।
तत्र भीमैर्लोकपुरुषैः पीड्यन्ते भोगपर्यन्तम् ॥८४॥

śāstraviruddhācaraṇātkṛṣṇaṁ ye karma vidadhate /
tatra bhīmairlokapuruṣaiḥ pīḍyante bhogaparyantam //84//

ये सकृदपि परमेशं शिवमेकाग्रेण चेतसा शरणं
यान्ति न ते नरकजुषः कृष्णं तेषां सुखाल्पतादायि ॥८५॥

ye sakṛdapi parameśaṁ śivamekāgreṇa cetasā śaraṇaṁ /
yānti na te narakajuṣaḥ kṛṣṇaṁ teṣāṁ sukhālpatādāyi //85//

अस्वतन्त्रस्य कर्तृत्वं नहि जातूपपद्यते ।
वस्तुतः सर्वभावानां कर्तेशानः परः शिवः ॥८६॥

asvatantrasya kartṛtvaṁ nahi jātūpapadyate /
vastutaḥ sarvabhāvānāṁ karteśānaḥ paraḥ śivaḥ //86//

तथा च तेषां हेतूनां संयोजनवियोजने ।
नियते शिव एवैकः स्वतंत्रः कर्तृतामियात् ॥८७॥

tathā ca teṣāṁ hetunāṁ saṁyojanaviyojane /
niyate śiva evaikaḥ svatantraḥ kartṛtāmiyāt //87//

बहवो गुरवः सन्ति शिष्यवित्तापहारकाः ।
दुर्लभोऽयं गुरुर्देवि शिष्यसन्तापहारकः ॥८८॥

bahavo guravaḥ santi śiṣyavittāpahārakāḥ /
durlabho'yaṁ gururdevi śiṣyasantāpahārakaḥ //88//

श्रीमत्सदाशिवपदेऽपि महोग्रकाली
भीमोत्कटभ्रुकुटिरेष्यति भङ्गभूमिः ।
इत्याकलय्य परमां स्थितिमेत्य काल-
सङ्कर्षिणीं भगवतीं हठतोऽधितिष्ठेत् ॥८९॥

śrīmatsadāśivapade'pi mahograkālī
bhīmotkaṭabhrukuṭireṣyati bhaṅgabhūmiḥ /
ityākalayya paramāṁ sthitimetya kāla-
saṅkarṣinīṁ bhagavatīṁ haṭhato'dhitiṣṭhet //89//
(verse from the Amṛteśvara Pūja)

तन्मध्ये तु परादेवी दक्षिणे च परापरा ।
अपरा वामश्रृंगे तु मध्यश्रृंगोर्ध्वतः श्रृणु ॥
या सा संकर्षिणीकाली परातीता व्यवस्थिता ।

tanmadhye tu parādevī dakṣine ca parāparā /
aparā vāmaśṛṅge tu madhyasṛṅgo'rdhvatah śṛṇu //
yā sā saṁkarṣinī kālī parātītā vyavasthitā /

Krama Stotra
Hymn to the Twelve Kālīs

कौलार्णवानन्दघनोर्मिरूपा-
मुन्मेषमेषोभयभाजमन्तः ।
निलीयते नीलकुलालये या तां

सृष्टिकालीं सततं नमामि ॥ १ ॥

kaulārṇav-ānanda-ghanormi-rūpām-
unmeṣameṣobhayabhajamantaḥ /
nilīyate nīlakulālaye yā tāṁ
sṛṣṭikālīṁ satataṁ namāmi //1//

I pay eternal homage to Sṛṣṭikālī, who remains hidden in the abode of the totality of the objective world. Similar to a blissful wave or tide in the ocean of consciousness, it is she who enjoys in her own Self the creation and dissolution of the universe.

महाविनोदार्पितमातृचक्र-
वीरेन्द्रकासृग्रसपानसक्ताम् ।
रक्तीकृतां च प्रलयात्यये तां
नमामि विश्वाकृतिरक्तकालीम् ॥ २ ॥

mahā-vinodārpita-mātṛ-cakra-
vīrendrakā-sṛg-rasa-pāna-saktam /
raktī-kṛtāṁ ca pralayātyaye tāṁ
namāmi viśvā-kṛti-rakta-kālīm //2//

Salutations to Raktakālī, who appears as the universe. With the host of *siddha*s and *yoginī*s, it is she who is fond of quaffing the blood-nectar of the subjective wheel which is offered to her with excessive happiness when dissolution has totally disappeared!

वाजिद्वयस्वीकृतवातचक्र-
प्रक्रान्तसंघट्टगमागमस्थाम् ।

शुचिर्ययास्तंगमितोर्चिषा तां
शान्तां नमामि स्थितिनाशकालीम् ॥ ३ ॥

vājidvaya-svī-kṛtavāta-cakra-
prakrānta-saṁghaṭṭa-gamāgamasthām /
śucir-yayāstaṁ-gamitorciṣā tāṁ
śāntāṁ namāmi sthitināśa kālīm //3//

I pay homage to that well-appeased Sthitināśakālī, who absorbs the destroyer. Established in the unifying center of the conscious and unconscious, which begins at the wheel of life-force (*prāṇān*), she makes her own both the outward and inward breath (*prāṇa-apāna*). By her flame, the pure light of subjective awareness sets in the horizon.

सर्वार्थसंकर्षणसंयमस्य-
यमस्य यन्तुर्जगतो यमाय ।
वपुर्महाग्रासविलासरागा-
त्संकर्षयन्तीं प्रणमामि कालीम् ॥ ४ ॥

sarvartha saṁkarṣaṇa-saṁyamasya-
yamasya yantur jagato yamāya /
vapur mahāgrāsa vilāsarāgāt
saṁkarṣayan-tīṁ praṇamāmi kālīm //4//

I salute Yamakālī, goddess of the great display and the great swallowing. It is she who attracts everything into herself by extracting the essence of the ruler of Yama (viz., thoughts) who is himself ruling the withdrawal of everything.

उन्मन्यनन्ता निखिलार्थगर्भा
या भावसंहारनिमेषमेति ।
सदोदिता सत्युदयाय शून्यां
संहारकालीं मुदितां नमामि ॥५॥

unmanyanantā nikhilārtha-garbhā
yā bhāva saṁhāra nimeṣameti /
sadoditā satyudayāya śūnyāṁ
saṁhāra kālīṁ muditām namāmi //5//

I bow to the energy of the perfect void, the joyful Saṁhārakālī, goddess of destruction! Infinite, beyond mind, containing in herself everything, eternally rising, she, to rise anew, disappears in the form of objective destruction.

ममेत्यहंकारकलाकलाप-
विस्फारहर्षोद्धतगर्वमृत्युः ।
ग्रस्तो यया घस्मरसंविदं तां
नमामि कालोदितमृत्युकालीम् ॥६॥

mamety-ahaṁkāra-kalākalāpa-
visphā raharṣoddhata-garva-mṛtyuḥ /
grasto yayā ghasmara saṁvidaṁ tāṁ
namāmi kālodita mṛtyu kālīm //6//

Obeisance to that voracious consciousness known as Mṛtyukālī, who beyond time, limitation rises unexpectedly. She devours death, which appears in the form of arrogance inflamed by a joyful excitement expanding itself to all ego-activities when the notion of ownership expresses itself in the idea, “This is mine.”

विश्वं महाकल्पविरामकल्प-
भवान्तभीमभ्रुकुटिभ्रमन्त्या ।
याश्नात्यनन्तप्रभवार्चिषा तां
नमामि भद्रां शुभभद्रकालीम् ॥७॥

viśvaṁ mahākalpa-virāma-kalpa-
bhavānta-bhīma-bhrukuṭi-bhramantyā /
yāśnātya-nanta-prabhavār-ciṣā tāṁ
namāmi bhadrāṁ śubha-bhadra-kālīm //7//

I bow before the pure and auspicious Rudrakālī, furiously frowning in her dance of destruction. By the flame of her unlimited power, she devours in one gulp the entire universe at the time of total dissolution (*mahākalpa*).

मार्तण्डमापीतपतङ्गचक्रं
पतङ्गवत्कालकलेन्धनाय ।
करोति या विश्वरसान्तकां तां
मार्तण्डकालीं सततं प्रणौमि ॥८॥

mārtaṇḍam-āpīta-pataṅga-cakraṁ
pataṅgavat-kāla-kalendhanāya /
karoti yā viśva-rasāntakāṁ tāṁ
mārtaṇḍakālīṁ satataṁ praṇaumi //8//

Salutations to Martāṇḍakālī, who, as the destroyer of the wheel of cognition, puts an end to all objective flavors. Desirous of consuming all worldly activities, she causes the twelve sun-gods, in the shape of the bird-wheel, to be completely consumed like a moth entering a raging fire.

अस्तोदितद्वादशभानुभाजि
यस्यां गता भर्गशिखा शिखेव ।
प्रशान्तधाम्नि द्युतिनाशमेति
तां नौम्यनन्तां परमार्ककालीम् ॥९॥

astodita-dvādaśa-bhānu-bhāji
yasyāṁ gatā bharga-śikhā śikheva /
praśānta-dhāmni dyuti-nāśam-eti
tāṁ naumyan-antāṁ paramārkakālīm //9//

I bow to that infinite Paramārkakālī, who, in her appeased flame, shares the twelve suns already consumed. It is in her that the ego (*ahaṁkāra*) succeeds in destroying its own light as an appeased flame in an appeased fire.

कालक्रमाक्रान्तदिनेशचक्र-
क्रोडीकृतान्ताग्निकलाप उग्रः ।
कालाग्निरुद्रो लयमेति यस्यां
तां नौमि कालानलरुद्रकालीम् ॥१०॥

kālakram-ākrānta-dineśa-cakra-
kroḍī-kṛtāntāgni-kalāpa ugraḥ /
kālāgni-rudro layameti yasyāṁ
tāṁ naumi kālānalarudrakālīm //10//

Obeisance to the fearful Kalāgnirudrakālī, who creates her own collection of internal fires when she overcomes temporal succession in the form of the previously digested sun-wheel. To this Kalāgnirudrakālī, in whom succession entirely dissolves, I bow down!

नक्तं महाभूतलये श्मशाने
दिग्खेचरीचक्रगणेन साकम् ।
कालीं महाकालमलं ग्रसन्तीं वन्दे
ह्यचिन्त्यामनिलानलाभाम् ॥ ११ ॥

naktaṁ mahābhūta-laye śmaśāne
digkhecarī-cakra-gaṇena sākam /
kālīṁ mahākālam alaṁ grasantīṁ vande
hyacintyām-anilā-nalā-bhām //11//

I bow to that inexpressible Mahākālakālī, who resides in the cremation ground where, during the night, all the five great elements are dissolved. As a fire powerfully excited by wind, she enthusiastically swallows the great lord of time (Mahākāla) along with the wheel of the energies governing the ten directions.

क्रमत्रयत्वाष्ट्रमरीचिचक्र-
सञ्चारचातुर्यतुरीयसत्ताम् ।
वन्दे महाभैरव घोर चण्ड-
कालीं कलाकाशशशाङ्ककान्तिं ॥ १२ ॥

kramatraya-tvāṣṭra-marīci-cakra-
sañcāra-cāturya-turīya-sattām /

vande mahābhairava ghora caṇḍa-
kālīṁ kalākāśa-śaśaśāṅka-kāntim //12//

Highest salutations to Mahābhairavaghoracaṇḍakālī, shining like the moon in the light of *kalākāśa* (the ether of God consciousness). She is the reality of the fourth state, *turya*, expert in spinning the wheel of the supreme sun, the rays of *prakāśa*. To this supreme goddess, weaver of the threefold succession of creating, protecting and destroying this entire universe, I constantly bow.

Additional verse from Kālīkā Stotra

अव्ययमकुलममेयं
विगलितसदसद्विवेककल्लोलम् ।
जयति प्रकाशविभव-
स्फीतं काल्याः परं धाम ॥

avyayam-akulam-ameyaṁ
vigalita-sadasad-viveka-kallolam /
jayati prakāśa-vibhava-
sphītaṁ kālyāḥ paraṁ dhāma //

O divine Mother, glory be to Thy supreme state of Kālī which shines intensely by its own light and energy. You are that undifferentiated, indestructible, infinite state in which the waves of discrimination of existence and non-existence have entirely disappeared.

Twelve Kālīs in Kashmir Shaivism from Tantrāloka, Āhnika Four.

The twelve Kālīs have their respective functions of creation (*sṛṣṭi*), protection (*sthiti*), destruction (*saṁhāra*), and *turya* (*anākhya*), in the three states of objectivity (*prameya*), cognition (*pramāṇa*), and subjectivity (*pramātṛ*).

Four Kālīs in the objective cycle (*prameya*)
1. Sṛṣṭikālī: creation in the objective cycle
2. Raktakālī: protection in the objective cycle
3. Sthitināśakālī: destruction in the objective cycle
4. Yamakālī: *anākhya* in the objective cycle

Four Kālīs in the cognitive cycle (*pramāṇa*)
5. Saṁhārakālī: creation in the cognitive cycle
6. Mṛtyukālī: protection in the cognitive cycle
7. Bhadrakālī: destruction in the cognitive cycle
8. Martāṇḍakālī: *anākhya* in the cognitive cycle

Four Kālīs in the subjective cycle (*pramātṛ*)
9. Paramārkakālī: creation in the subjective cycle
10. Kalāgnirudrakālī: protection in the subjective cycle
11. Mahākālakāl: destruction in the subjective cycle
12. Mahābhairavaghoracaṇḍakālī: *anākhya* in the subjective cycle.

"And the purpose of twelve Kālīs," Swamiji tells us, "is to find that state [of *anākhya*] in each and every state. In *sṛṣṭi* (creation) also, you have to find *anākhya*. These twelve Kālīs are the explanation of *anākhya cakra* only. It is not the explanation of objectivity or cognitivity or subjectivity. You have to find that real transcendental state of nothingness in each and every act." The explanation of the twelvefold energies is the explanation of the kingdom of Trika. This is the kingdom of Trika *Śāstra*.

Anuttarāṣṭikā of Abhinavagupta
Eight Verses on the Supreme (Anuttara)

संक्रामोऽत्र न भावना न च काथायुक्तिर्न चर्चा न च
ध्यानं वा न च धारणा न च जपाभ्यासप्रयासो न च ।
तत्किं नाम सुनिश्चितं वद परं सत्यं च तच्छ्रूयतां
न त्यागी न परिग्रही भज सुखं सर्वं यथावस्थितः ॥ १ ॥

saṁkrāmo'tra na bhāvanā na ca kathā-yuktir na carcā na ca
dhyānaṁ vā na ca dhāraṇā na ca japā-bhyāsa prayāso na ca /
tatkiṁ nāma suniścitaṁ vada paraṁ satyaṁ ca tacchrūyatāṁ
na tyāgī na parigrahī bhaja sukhaṁ sarvaṁ yathāva-sthitaḥ //1//

In this highest state of supreme God consciousness (*anuttara*), there is no need of spiritual progress, no contemplation, no art of expression, no investigation, no meditation, no concentration, no recitation, exertion or practice. Tell me then, what is the supreme and well-ascertained truth? Listen indeed to this! Neither abandon nor accept anything, enjoy everything, remain as you are!

संसारो ऽस्ति न तत्त्वतस्तनुभृतां बन्धस्य वार्तैव का
बन्धो यस्य न जातु तस्य वितथा मुक्तस्य मुक्तिक्रिया ।
मिथ्यामोहकृदेष रज्जुभुजगच्छायापिशाचभ्रमो
मा किंचित् त्यज मा गृहाण विहर स्वस्थो यथावस्थितः
॥ २ ॥

saṁsāro'sti na tattvatastanubhṛtāṁ bandhasya vārtaiva kā
bandho yasya na jātu tasya vitathā muktasya muktikriyā /

mithyāmohakṛdeṣa rajjubhujagacchāyāpiśācabhramo
mā kiṁcit tyaja mā gṛhāṇa vilasa svastho yathāvasthitaḥ //2//

In reality, there is no such thing as birth and death, so how can the question arise of bondage for living beings? There never was any such bondage for the one who is entirely free, and therefore, to struggle for liberation is useless and nothing more than delusion, like a dark shadow mistaken for a demon, or a rope seen as a snake. It is all based on deceitful perception which has no substance. Neither abandon nor accept anything, remain as you are, well-established in your own Self.

पूजापूजकपूज्यभेदसरणिः केयं कथानुत्तरे
संक्रामः किल कस्य केन विदधे को वा प्रवेशक्रमः ।
मायेयं न चिदद्वयात्परतया भिन्नाप्यहो वर्तते
सर्वं स्वानुभवस्वभावविमलं चिन्तां वृथा मा कृथाः ॥ ३ ॥

pūjāpūjaka pūjya bheda-saraṇiḥ keyaṁ kathānuttare
saṁkrāmaḥ kila kasya kena vidadhe ko vā praveśa kramaḥ /
māyeyaṁ na cidadvayātparatayā bhinnāpyaho vartate
sarvaṁ svānubhava svabhāva vimalaṁ cintāṁ vṛthā mā kṛthāḥ //3//

In the oneness of that supreme state of *anuttara*, what talk can there be, and what differentiated path of the adorer, the adored and the adoration? To whom and by what means could a progression function, or what could constitute the succession of penetrating into the Self? Wonder of wonders! Though it appears differentiated, this illusion is no other than consciousness–one without a second. Everything is nothing but the pure essence of your own Self-experience, so why worry in vain?

आनन्दोऽत्र न वित्तमद्यमदवन्नैवाङ्गनासङ्गवत्
दीपार्केन्दुकृतप्रभाप्रकरवन् नैव प्रकाशोदयः ।
हर्षः संभृतभेदमुक्तिसुखभूर्भारावतारोपमः
सर्वाद्वैतपदस्य विस्मृतनिधेः प्राप्तिः प्रकाशोदयः ॥ ४ ॥

ānando'tra na vittam adyamadavannaivāṅganāsaṅgavat
dīpārkendukṛta prabhā prakaravan naiva prakaśodayaḥ /
harṣaḥ saṁbhṛtabhedamuktisukhabhūrbhārāvatāropamaḥ
sarvā dvaita padasya vismṛta nidheḥ prāptiḥ prakāśodayaḥ //4//

One cannot compare the bliss of this state to the intoxication of wealth or wine, nor to the union with a beloved woman. And the brilliant flow of light is unlike the collection of rays from a lamp, the sun or the moon. This excessive joy of the Self is comparable only to the weight of that blissful state which descends when one gets liberated from all differentiation. The flow of this supreme consciousness is the state of universal oneness, which is nothing other than your own treasure-abode that you had temporarily forgotten.

रागद्वेषसुखासुखोदयलयाहंकारदैन्यादयो
ये भावाः प्रविभान्ति विश्ववपुषो भिन्नस्वभावा न ते ।
व्यक्तिं पश्यसि यस्य यस्य सहसा तत्तत्तदेकात्मता
संविद्रूपम् अवेक्ष्य किं न रमसे तद्भावनानिर्भरः ॥५॥

rāgadveśasukhāsukhodayalayāhaṅkāradainyādayo
ye bhāvāḥ pravibhānti viśvavapuṣo bhinnasvabhāvā na te /
vyaktiṁ paśyasi yasya yasya sahasā tattattadekātmatā
saṁvidrūpam avekṣya kiṁ na ramase tadbhāvanānirbharaḥ //5//

Attraction and repulsion, pleasure and pain, rising and setting, self-confidence and depression, all these states with which the universe is formed shine as mutually different but in reality they are not. Whenever you perceive the specificity of some thing, at that very moment you should perceive the essence of your own consciousness as one with it. Why not take delight in the fullness of that awareness?

पूर्वाभावभवक्रिया हि सहसा भावाः सदास्मिन्भवे
मध्याकारविकारसङ्करवतां तेषां कुतः सत्यता ।
निःसत्ये चपले प्रपञ्चनिचये स्वप्नभ्रमे पेशले
शङ्कातङ्कलङ्कयुक्तिकलनानीतःप्रबुद्धो भव ॥६॥

pūrvābhāva bhavakriyā hi sahasā bhāvāḥ sadāsminbhave
madhyākāra vikāra saṅkara-vatāṁ teṣāṁ kutaḥ satyatā /
niḥsatye capale prapañca nicaye svapna bhrame peśale
śaṅkātaṅkakalaṅkayuktikalanātītaḥ prabuddho bhava //6//

In this world, the totality of objects appear eternally in the present moment. The activity of universality has no previous or future existence. Differentiated action is an illusion based on the unlawful pervasion of an intermediate state which is unreal, transient, fraudulent, just like a heap of appearances in the illusion of a dream. Remain above these defects which have been wrongfully forged by the stigma of doubts, hence be awakened!

भावानां न समुद्भवोऽस्ति सहजस्त्वद्भाविता भान्त्यमी
निःसत्या अपि सत्यतामनुभवभ्रान्त्या भजन्ति क्षणम् ।
त्वत्सङ्कल्पज एष विश्वमहिमा नास्त्यस्य जन्मान्यतः
तस्मात्त्वं विभवेन भासि भुवनेष्वेकोप्यनेकात्मकः ॥७॥

bhāvānāṁ na samudbhavo'sti sahajastvad bhāvitā bhāntyamī
niḥsatyā api satyatāmanubhavabhrāntyā bhajanti kṣaṇam /
tvatsaṅkalpaja eṣa viśva mahimā nāstyasya janmānyataḥ
tasmāttvaṁ vibhavena bhāsi bhuvaneṣvekopyanekātmakaḥ //7//

For the insentient, there is no outflow of objective things, for those are manifested only when experienced by thee. Though deprived of reality, they share reality in one instant through one's erroneous perception. Thus the greatness of this universe arises from your own imagination. It does not take birth from anything else. Therefore, you alone shine in all these worlds, and though one, you become many by your own glory!

यत्सत्यं यदसत्यमल्पबहुलं नित्यं न नित्यं च यत्
यन्मायामलिनं यदात्मविमलं चिद्दर्पणे राजते ।
तत्सर्वं स्वविमर्शसंविदुदयाद् रूपप्रकाशात्मकं ज्ञात्वा
स्वानुभवाधिरूढमहिमा विश्वेश्वरत्वं भज ॥८॥

yatsatyaṁ yad asatyamalpabahulaṁ nityaṁ na nityaṁ ca yat
yan māyāmalinaṁ yadātmavimalaṁ ciddarpaṇe rājate /
tatsarvaṁ svavimarśasaṁvidudayād rūpaprakāśātmakaṁ
jñātvā svānubhavā dhirūḍhamahimā viśveśvaratvaṁ bhaja //8//

Real or unreal, small or plentiful, eternal or momentary, what is colored by the illusion of differentiation and what is pure in one's own Self, in reality, this universe, rising from your own consciousness and becoming one with your essence, appears glorified in the mirror of Consciousness.

Having ascertained the sublimity of the universe and having understood the greatness of establishing one's own Self-experience, enjoy universal sovereignty.

Bhairava Stotra of Abhinavagupta
Hymn to Bhairava

व्याप्तचराचरभावविशेषं चिन्मयमेकमनन्तमनादिम् ।
भैरवनाथमनाथशरण्यं तन्मयचित्ततया हृदि वंदे ॥ १ ॥

vyāpta carācara, bhāva viśeṣaṁ cinmayam ekam, anantam anādim /
bhairava-nātham, anātha śaraṇyaṁ tanmaya citta, tayā hṛdi vande //1//

I, Abhinavagupta, with one-pointed devotion, am praying to that supreme all-pervading Lord Śiva, who is himself present in each and everything that exists, and who, through realization, reveals himself as the one limitless Bhairavanātha, the protector of the helpless.

त्वन्मयमेतदशेषमिदानीं
भाति मम त्वदनुग्रहशक्त्या ।
त्वं च महेश! सदैव ममात्मा
स्वात्ममयं मम तेन समस्तम् ॥ २ ॥

tvanmayametad, aśeṣhamidānīṁ
bhāti mama tvad, anugrahaśaktyā /
tvam ca maheśha! sadaiva mamātmā
svātmamayaṁ mama, tena samastam //2//

By the energy of your grace, it has been revealed to me that this vibrating universe is your own existence. Thus, O Lord Śiva, this realization has come to me that you are my own soul and as such, this universe is my own expression and existence.

स्वात्मनि विश्वगते त्वयि नाथे तेन न संसृतिभीतिःकथाऽस्ति।
सत्स्वपि दुर्धरदुःखविमोहत्रासविधायिषु कर्मगणेषु ॥ ३ ॥

svātmani viśva, gate tvayi nāthe tena na saṁsṛti, bhītiḥ kathāsti /
sat svapi durdhara, duḥkha vimoha trāsa vidhāyiṣhu, karma gaṇeṣu //3//

O possessor of everything, though your devotees bound by *karma* and conditioning of mind are caught in the net of destiny that arouses troubles and bondage, still they are not afraid of the fret and fever of this world. Having realized this universe as your own existence, they are not afraid of worldly difficulties because fear exists only when there is someone else to inflict it. But when there is none other than you, how can fear arise?

अन्तक! मां प्रति मा दृशमेनां क्रोधकरालतमां विदधीहि ।
शङ्करसेवनचिन्तनधीरो भीषणभैरवशक्तिमयोऽस्मि ॥ ४ ॥

antaka! māṁ prati, mā dṛśamenāṁ krodha karāla, tamāṁ vida dhīhi /
śaṅkara sevana, cintana dhīro bhīṣaṇa bhairava, śakti mayo'smi //4//

O angel of death, do not look towards me with wrathful and frightening eyes as I am always absorbed in the worship of Lord Śiva. Through constant devotion, meditation and reflection, I have become steadfast and courageous, one with the energy of the terrifying Bhairava. Thus, your dreadful and frightening looks can do me no harm.

इत्थमुपोढभवन्मयसंविद्दीधितिदारितभूरितमिस्त्रः ।
मृत्युयमान्तककर्मपिशाचैनाथ! नमोऽस्तु न जातु बिभेमि
॥ ५ ॥

ittham upoḍha, bhavan maya saṁvit dīdhiti dārita, bhūri tamisraḥ /
mṛtyur yamāntaka, karma piśācair nātha namostu, na jātu bibhemi //5//

O Lord Bhairava, I offer salutations to you who has awakened me to the realization that everything in existence is you alone. As a result of this awakening, the darkness of my mind has been destroyed and I am neither frightened of the evil family of demons nor am I afraid of Yama, the fearful lord of death.

प्रोदितसत्यविबोधमरीचिप्रोक्षितविश्वपदार्थसतत्त्वः ।
भावपरामृतनिर्भरपूर्णे त्वय्यऽहमात्मनि निर्वृत्तिमेमि ॥६॥

prodita satya, vibodha marīci prokṣita viśva, padārtha satattvaḥ /
bhāva parāmṛta, nirbhara pūrṇe tvayya'ham ātmani, nirvṛttim emi //6//

O Lord Śiva, it is through your existence, revealed to me by real knowledge, that I realize all attachments and all that exists in this universe is activated by you. It is by this awakening that my mind becomes saturated with immortal devotion and I experience supreme bliss.

मानसगोचरमेति यदैव क्लेशदशाऽतनुतापविधात्री ।
नाथ! तदैव मम त्वदभेदस्तोत्रपराऽमृतवृष्टिरुदेति ॥७॥

mānasa gocaram, eti yadaiva kleśa daśā'tanu, tāpa vidhātrī /
nātha! tadaiva, mama tvadabheda stotra parā'mṛta, vṛṣṭi rudeti //7//

O Lord, sometimes I feel misery which arouses torment in my mind, but at that same moment, blessed by a shower of your grace, a clean and clear vision of my oneness with you arises, the impact of which my mind feels appeased.

शङ्कर! सत्यमिदं व्रतदानस्नानतपो भवतापविनाशि ।
तावकशास्त्रपराऽमृतचिन्ता स्यन्दति चेतसि निर्वृत्तिधाराम्
॥८॥

śaṅkara satyam, idaṁ vrata dāna snāna tapo bhava, tāpa vināśi /
tāvaka śāstra, parā'mṛta cintā syandati cetasi, nirvṛtti dhārā //8//

O Lord Śiva, it is said that through charity, ritual bath and the practices of penance, the troubles of worldly existence subside, but even more than this, by remembrance of the sacred *śāstra*s and your words alone, the current of immortality like a stream of peace enters my heart.

नृत्यति गायति हृष्यति गाढं
संविदियं मम भैरवनाथ! ।
त्वां प्रियमाप्य सुदर्शनमेकं
दुर्लभमन्यजनैः समयज्ञम् ॥९॥

nṛtyati gāyati, hṛṣyati gāḍhaṁ
saṁvid iyaṁ mama, bhairavanātha! /
tvāṁ priyam āpya, sudarśanam ekaṁ
durlabham anya, janaiḥ sama yajñam //9//

O Lord Bhairava, through my utmost faith I have perceived you in the unique sacrifice of oneness, which otherwise is not possible though performing mountains of rituals. Being filled with your presence, my consciousness intensely dances and sings, enjoying its own ecstacy.

वसुरसपौषे कृष्णदशम्यामभिनवगुप्तः स्तवमिदमकरोत् ।
येन विभुर्भवमरुसन्तापं शमयति झटिति जनस्य
दयालुः ॥ १० ॥

vasu rasapauṣe, kṛṣṇa daśam yām abhinavaguptaḥ, stavam imam akarot /
yena vibhur bhava, maru san tāpaṁ śamayati jhaṭiti, janasya dayāluḥ //10//

O compassionate Lord, under the influence of your glory and for the benefit of your worshipers, I, Abhinavagupta, have composed this hymn. By meditation and recitation of this hymn, within a moment that merciful Lord Bhairava destroys the torments and sufferings springing from this wilderness of *saṁsāra*.

DEHASTHADEVATĀCAKRA STOTRA OF ABHINAVAGUPTA

HYMN TO THE GODS AND GODDESSES RESIDING IN ONE'S OWN BODY

असुरसुरवृन्दवन्दितमभिमतवरवितरणे निरतम् ।
दर्शनशताग्र्यपूज्यं प्राणतनुं गणपतिं वन्दे ॥ १ ॥

asura-sura-vṛnda-vanditam abhimata-vara-vitaraṇe niratam /
darśana-śatāgrya-pūjyaṁ prāṇa-tanuṁ gaṇapatiṁ vande //1//

Salutations to Gaṇeśa, the first to be worshipped in all hymns and rituals. As the embodiment of *prāṇa* (breath), he is adored by gods, goddesses and demons alike. I pray to Gaṇeśa who is soft in bestowing boons, that he may allow me to enter in the temple of my own body.

वरवीरयोगिनीगणसिद्धावलिपूजितांघ्रियुगलम् ।
अपहृतविनयिजनार्तिं वटुकमपानाभिधं वन्दे ॥२॥

vara-vīra-yoginī-gaṇa-siddhā-vali-pūjitāṁ-ghri-yugalam /
apahṛta-vina-yijanārtiṁ vaṭukam apānābhidhaṁ vande //2//

I pay homage to Vaṭukanātha, who also resides at the door of this temple of my body, in the form of *apāna*, the in-going breath. Whose divine feet are worshipped by *vīra*s (heroes), *siddha*s (male saints) and *yoginī*s (female saints), who is capable of removing all knots and doubts in the minds of disciples who have taken refuge at the masters feet, to Vaṭukanātha, I offer salutations.

आत्मीयविषयभोगैरिन्द्रियदेव्यः सदा हृदम्भोजे ।
अभिपूजयन्ति यं तं चिन्मयमानन्दभैरवं वन्दे ॥३॥

ātmīya-viṣaya-bhogair-indriya-devyaḥ sadā hṛdam-bhoje /
abhi-pūja-yanti yaṁ taṁ cin-mayam-ānanda-bhairavaṁ vande //3//

I bow to that ever-blissful Bhairavanātha (Lord Śiva) residing in the center of the lotus of my heart. The goddesses of the *indriya*s (organs) are constantly in search of pleasant sounds, soft touch, beautiful forms, delicious tastes, and fragrant smells, which they offer at the feet of their master, Bhairavanātha.

यद्धीबलेन विश्वं भक्तानां शिवपथं भाति ।
तमहमवधानरूपं सद्गुरुममलं सदा वन्दे ॥४॥

yad-dhībalena viśvaṁ bhaktānāṁ śiva-pathaṁ bhāti /
tamaham-avadhāna-rūpaṁ sadgurum-amalaṁ sadā vande //4//

I bow to that absolutely pure and clean master residing in the temple of my body. Through constant devotion, my master has bestowed upon me the strength of intellectual understanding by which I experience this whole universe consisting of pain, pleasure and sorrow as a pathway towards Śiva. Salutations to that master, the embodiment of awareness (*vimarśa*), the real means of perceiving Lord Śiva in the lotus of my heart.

उदयावभासचर्वणलीलां विश्वस्य या करोत्यनिशम् ।
आनन्दभैरवीं तां विमर्शरूपामहं वन्दे ॥५॥

udayāvabhāsa-carvaṇa-līlāṁ viśvasya yā karotyaniśam /
ānanda-bhairavīṁ tāṁ vimarśa-rūpāṁ ahaṁ vande //5//

I bow to goddess, Pārvatī, who creates, maintains and destroys this universe in her own Self. Inseparable from Śiva, she is the blissful *ānanda*-Bhairavī. Being filled with the energy of awareness (*vimarśa*), she resides near the seat of her master in the lotus of my heart.

अर्चयति भैरवं या निश्चयकुसुमैः सुरेशपत्रस्था ।
प्रणमामि बुद्धिरूपां ब्रह्माणीं तामहं सततम् ॥६॥

arcayati bhairavaṁ yā niścaya-kusumaiḥ sureśa-patrasthā /
praṇamāmi buddhi-rūpāṁ brahmāṇīṁ tāmahaṁ satatam //6//

Salutations to the goddess of the intellect, Brahmaṇī. Residing in the eastern direction, she confirms all perceptions of the outside world and offers them like flowers to Lord Śiva seated in the heart-lotus of my heart.

कुरुते भैरवपूजामनलदलस्थाऽभिमानकुसुमैर्या ।
नित्यमहंकृतिरूपां वन्दे तां शाम्भवीमम्बाम् ॥७॥

kurute bhairava-pūjām-aṇala ḍalasthā'bhimāna-kusumairyā /
nityam-ahaṁ-kṛti-rūpāṁ vande tāṁ śāmbhavīm-ambām //7//

I bow to goddess, Śāṁbhavī, the embodiment of *ahaṁkāra* (ego), who eternally worships Lord Śiva by offering flowers of I-ness to his lotus feet.

विदधाति भैरवार्चां दक्षिणदलगा विकल्पकुसुमैर्या ।
नित्यं मनः स्वरूपां कौमारीं तामहं वन्दे ॥८॥

vidadhāti bhairavārcāṁ dakṣiṇa-dalagā vikalpa-kusumairyā /
nityaṁ manaḥ svarūpāṁ kaumārīṁ tām-ahaṁ vande //8//

Homage to goddess, Kaumārī, the embodiment of mind. Situated in the south, it is she who offers the flowers of ideas and notions (*vikalpa*s) to Lord Śiva.

नैर्ऋतदलगा भैरवमर्चयते शब्दकुसुमैर्या ।
प्रणमामि श्रुतिरूपां नित्यं तां वैष्णवीं शक्तिम् ॥९॥

nairṛta-dalagā bhairavam arcayete-śabda-kusumairyā /
praṇamāmi śruti-rūpāṁ nityaṁ tāṁ vaiṣṇavīṁ śaktiṁ //9//

I bow to that eternal and all-pervading goddess, Vaiṣṇavī, situated on the point of *nairṛti* (southwest). Collecting a garland of beautiful sounds, she worships Bhairavanātha on the lotus of my heart.

पश्चिमदिग्दलसंस्था हृदयहरैः स्पर्शकुसुमैर्या ।
तोषयति भैरवं तां त्वग्रूपधरां नमामि वाराहीम् ॥ १० ॥

paścima-digdala-saṁsthā hṛdaya-haraiḥ sparśa-kusumairyā /
toṣayati bhairavaṁ tāṁ tvag-rūpa-dharāṁ namāmi vārāhīm //10//

Salutations to goddess, Vārāhī. Situated in the west, she collects all good sensations of touch to satisfy Lord Bhairava residing in the lotus of my heart.

वरतररूपविशेषैर्मारुतदिग्दलनिषण्णदेहा या ।
पूजयति भैरवं तामिन्द्राणीं दृक्तनुं वन्दे ॥ ११ ॥

varatara-rūpa-viśeṣair māruta-digdala-niṣaṇṇa-dehā yā /
pūjayati bhairavaṁ tām indrāṇīṁ dṛk-tanuṁ vande //11//

I bow to goddess, Indrāṇī, who is established in the northwest, the abode of the Māruts (wind gods, *vāyu*). As the embodiment of the vibrating force of sight, she worships Bhairava with all forms which are pleasing to the eye.

धनपतिकिसलयनिलया या नित्यं विविधषड्रसाहारैः ।
पूजयति भैरवं तां जिह्वाभिख्यां नमामि चामुण्डाम् ॥ १२ ॥

dhanapati-kisalaya-nilayā yā nityaṁ vividha-ṣaḍ-rasā-hāraiḥ /
pūjayati bhairavaṁ tāṁ jihvābhikhyāṁ namāmi cāmuṇḍām //12//

Salutations to Cāmuṇḍā, established in the northern abode of the lord of treasure (Kubera). I bow to goddess, Cāmuṇḍā, whose tongue is always protruding because she is fond of tasting the sixfold *rasa*s (tastes) and offering them to Bhairava in my heart.

ईशादलस्था भैरवमर्चयते परिमलैर्विचित्रैर्या ।
प्रणमामि सर्वदा तां घ्राणाभिख्यां महालक्ष्मीम् ॥ १३ ॥

īśa-dalasthā bhairavam-arcayate parimalair-vicitrairyā /
praṇamāmi sarvadā tāṁ ghrāṇābhikhyāṁ mahā lakṣmīṁ //13//

I bow to Lakṣmī, goddess of wealth, who is fond of perfume and all good scents, and who is situated in the abode of Iśāna (northeast). To Mahā Lakṣmī, who embodies the sense of smell, and who worships Bhairavanātha with various perfumes and scents, I eternally bow.

षड्दर्शनेषु पूज्यं षड्त्रिंशत्तत्त्वसंवलितम् ।
आत्माभिख्यं सततं क्षेत्रपतिं सिद्धिदं वन्दे ॥ १४ ॥

ṣaḍ-darśaneṣu pūjyaṁ ṣaḍ-triṁśat-tattva-saṁvalitam /
ātmābhikhyaṁ satataṁ kṣetrapatiṁ siddhidaṁ vande //14//

Salutations to Kṣetrapāla, who is situated in the aura of my body, adored in the six systems of philosophy, the embodiment of the thirty-six elements. To Kṣetrapāla, the *ātmā* or individual being, whose duty it is to protect me on all sides, I bow down.

संस्फुरदनुभवसारं सर्वान्तः सततसन्निहितम् ।
नौमि सदोदितमित्थं निजदेहगदेवताचक्रम् ॥ १५ ॥

saṁsphurad-anubhava-sāraṁ sarvāntaḥ satatasan-nihitam /
naumi sadoditam-itthaṁ nija-dehaga-devatā cakram //15//

Finally, I bow collectively to all the divine gods and goddesses who are always present, always shining in the temple of my own body.

Abhinavagupta composed these fifteen verses of the *Dehastadevatācakra Stotra* to help the sincere *sādhaka* (aspirant) understand that their body is divine, it is not something bad. Your own body is divine, so you should always worship your body with good things. In this way, all the gatherings of gods and goddesses, which are situated in your body, can be perceived, can be achieved, and can be known by your own intellectual way of thinking.

इति श्रीमाचार्याभिनवगुप्तपादविरचितं
देहस्थदेवताचक्रस्तोत्रम् ।
इति शिवम् ।

Sixteen Amṛtas (Nectars)

अथ श्रीरुद्रामृतबीजसमुद्भावः ।

atha śrīrudrāmṛtabījasamudbhāvaḥ /

(अ) (अमृतः)

(*a*) (*amṛtaḥ*)

(Only Nectar)

अमृतमनन्तमनुत्तरमघोरषोडशकशक्तिचक्रगतम् ।
औन्मनसपदनिरूढिप्रथमोपोद्घातकं वन्दे ॥ १ ॥

amṛtamanantamanuttaram-aghoraṣoḍaśakaśakticakragatam /
aunmanasapadanirūḍhi-prathamopodghātakaṁ vande //1//

(आ) (अमृतपूर्णः)

(*ā*) (*amṛtapurṇaḥ*)

(Filled with Nectar)

आनन्दममृतपूर्णं सामनसे परपदे परं सत्यम् ।
घटितानुत्तरदृढतमनिरूढिभाजं शिवं वन्दे ॥ २ ॥

ānandamamṛtapūrṇaṁ sāmanase parapade paraṁ satyam /
ghaṭitānuttaradṛḍhatama-nirūḍhibhājaṁ śivaṁ vande //2//

(इ) (अमृताभः)

(*i*) (*amṛtābhaḥ*)

(Just like Nectar)

इच्छाशक्तिसुनिर्भरममृताभमनन्तभुवनजननपटुम् ।
वन्दे स्वशक्तिलहरीबहलितभैरवपरानन्दम् ॥ ३ ॥

icchāśaktisunirbharam-amṛtābhamanantabhuvanajananapaṭum /
vande svaṣaktilaharī-bahalitabhairavaparānandam //3//

(ई) (अमृतद्रवः)

(*ī*) (*amṛtadravaḥ*)

(Who flows out Nectar or who is soaked in Nectar)

ईश्वरमशेषतापप्रशमनममृतद्रवं सदा वन्दे ।
अप्रतिघातिस्वेच्छाविकासविश्रान्तममृतकरमौलिम् ॥ ४ ॥

īśvaramaśeṣatāpa-praśanamamṛtadravaṁ sadā vande /
apratighātisvecchā-vikāsaviśrāntamamṛtakaramaulim //4//

(उ) (अमृतौघः)

(*u*) (*amṛtaughaḥ*)

(Where there is confusion all-round with Nectar)

यदनुत्तरसम्बोधादानन्दविकस्वरेच्छाया पूर्णम् ।
ईश्वरमुन्मिषदमृतौघसुन्दरं तत्स्तुवे धाम ॥५॥

yadanuttarasambodhā-dānandavikasvarecchāyā pūrṇam /
īśvaramunmiṣadamṛtaugha-sundaraṁ tatstuve dhāma //5//

(ऊ) (अमृतोर्मिः)

(*ū*) (*amṛtormiḥ*)

(Tides of Nectar)

मानन्दघनेच्छाघटितेश्वरतोन्मिषत्समस्तोर्मिः ।
इत्युर्ल्लासतरङ्गितममृतोर्मिमहं चिदर्णवं वन्दे ॥६॥

ahamānandaghanecchā-ghaṭiteśvaratonmiṣatsamastormiḥ /
ityurllāsataraṅgitama-amṛtormimahaṁ cidarṇavaṁ vande //6//

(ऋ) (अमृतस्यन्दनः)

(*ṛ*) (*amṛtasyandanaḥ*)

(Who always vomits out Nectar)

स्वप्रसरप्रेङ्खितविलसदूर्मिसंक्षुभितचिद्रसापूरम् ।
अमृतस्यन्दनसारं भैरवसंविन्महार्णवं वन्दे ॥७॥

svaprasaraprenkhitavilasad-ūrmisaṁkṣubhitacidrasāpūram /
amṛtasyandanasāraṁ bhairavasaṁvinmahārṇavaṁ vande //7//

(ॠ) (अमृताङ्गः)

(*ṝ*) (*amṛtāṅgaḥ*)

(Whose limbs are made of Nectar)

पूर्वं यदनुत्तरममृतभूमिमासाद्य सप्तमीं कलनाम् ।
विश्राम्यति तत्प्रणमाम्यममृताङ्गदं परानन्दि ॥८॥

pūrvaṁ yadanuttaram-amṛtabhūmimāsādya saptamīṁ kalanām /
viśrāmyati tatpraṇamāmyam-amṛtāṅgadaṁ parānandi //8//

(ऌ) (अमृतवपुः)

(*ḷ*) (*amṛtavapuḥ*)

(Who is the embodiment of Nectar)

शिवममृतवपुषममृतकलाचतुष्टयतृतीयभागजुषम् ।
प्रणमामि भासयन्तं क्रमरहितेऽपि क्रमममनेकम् ॥९॥

śivamamṛtavapuṣam-amṛtakalācatuṣṭayatṛtīyabhāgajuṣam /
praṇmāmi bhāsayantaṁ kramarahite'pi kramamanekam //9//

(ॡ) (अमृतोद्गारः)

(*ḹ*) (*amṛtodgāraḥ*)

(Who screams always for Nectar/Who cries for Nectar)

संजीवनतुर्यकलाकलितविबोधं समस्तभावानाम् ।
दूषणविषशीर्णानाममृतोद्गारं शिवं वन्दे ॥१०॥

aṁjīvanaturyakalā-kalitavibodhaṁ samastabhāvānām /
dūṣaṇaviṣaśīrṇānām-amṛtodgāraṁ śivaṁ vande //10//

(ए) (अमृतास्यः)

(*e*) (*amṛtāsyaḥ*)

(Whose mouth is Nectar)

एकमनुत्तररूपात्प्रभृतित्रिकशक्तिपूरितानन्दम् ।
अमृतास्यमस्य जगतः प्रमाणभूतं शिवं वन्दे ॥ ११ ॥

ekamanuttararūpāt-prabhṛtitrikaśaktipūritānandam /
amṛtāsyamasya jagataḥ pramāṇabhūtaṁ śivaṁ vande //11//

(ऐ) (अमृततनुः)

(*ai*) (*amṛtatanuḥ*)

(Whose body is manufactured of Nectar)

ऐक्यपरमार्थकलया त्रिशक्तियुगघटितवैश्वरूप्यमहम् ।
अमृततनुमतनुबोधप्रसरमहाकारणं स्मरामि हरम् ॥ १२ ॥

aikyaparamārthakalayā triśaktiyugaghaṭitavaiśvarūpyamaham /
amṛtatanumatanubodha-prasaramahākāraṇaṁ smarāmi haram //12//

(ओ) (अमृतसेचनः)

(*o*) (*amṛtasecanaḥ*)

(Who sprays Nectar everywhere)

ओतप्रोतं सकलं विद्ध्वा स्वरसेन शिवमयीकुरुते ।
योऽनुत्तरधाम्न्युदयन्स्वयममृतनिषेचनं तमस्मि नतः ॥ १३ ॥

otaprotaṁ sakalaṁ viddhvā svarasena śivamayīkurute /
yo'nuttaradhāmnyudayan-svayamamṛitaniṣecanaṁ tamasmi nataḥ //13//

(औ) (अमृतमूर्तिः)

(*au*) (*amṛtamūrtiḥ*)

(Whose beauty (*rūpa*) is Nectar/whose formation is Nectar)

औषधमाधिव्याधिषु पाशत्रयशातनं त्रिशूलकरम् ।
वन्देऽहमममृतमूर्तिं पूर्णत्रिकशक्तिपरमार्थम् ॥ १४ ॥

auṣadhamādhivyādhiṣu pāśatrayaśātanaṁ triśūlakaram /
vande'hamamṛtamūrtiṁ pūrṇatrikaśaktiparamārtham //14//

(अँ) (अमृतेशः)

(*ṁ*) (*amṛteśaḥ*)

(Who is the governor of Nectar/who controls Nectar)

बैन्दवममृतरसमयं वन्दे योऽनुत्तरे निजे धाम्नि ।
पूर्णीभावयतितमाममृतेशं तं नमस्यामि ॥ १५ ॥

baindavamamṛtarasamayaṁ vande yo'nuttare nije dhāmni /
pūrṇībhāvayatitamām-amṛteśaṁ taṁ namasyāmi //15//

(अः) (सर्वामृतधरः)

(*aḥ*) (*sarvāmṛtadharaḥ*)

(Who beholds and sprinkles Nectar everywhere)

प्रसृतमनुत्तररूपादानन्दादिक्रमेण विश्वमदः ।
सर्वामृतधरमन्तर्बहुश्च विसृजन्तमभिवन्दे ॥ १६ ॥

prasṛtamanuttararūpād-ānandādikrameṇa viśvamadaḥ /
sarvāmṛtadharamantarbahuśca visṛjantamabhivande //16//

Bibliography

Published text of Lakshmanjoo Academy Book Series:

Essence of the Supreme Reality, Abhinavagupta's Paramārthasāra, with the commentary of Yogarāja, original video recording (Lakshmanjoo Academy Book Series, Los Angeles, 2015).

Bhagavad Gita in the Light of Kashmir Shaivism (with original video), ed. John Hughes (Lakshmanjoo Academy Book Series, Los Angeles, 2015).

Festival of Devotion and Praise, Shivastotrāvali, Hymns to Shiva by Utpaladeva, ed. John Hughes (Lakshmanjoo Academy Book Series, Los Angeles, 2015).

Kashmir Shaivism, The Secret Supreme, ed. John Hughes (Lakshmanjoo Academy Book Series, Los Angeles, 2015).

Light on Tantra in Kashmir Shaivism, Abhinavagupta's Tantrāloka, Vol. One, chapter 1, ed. John Hughes (Lakshmanjoo Academy, Los Angeles, 2017).

Light on Tantra in Kashmir Shaivism, Abhinavagupta's Tantrāloka, Vol. Two, chapters 2 & 3, Vol. Three, chapter 4, ed. John Hughes (Lakshmanjoo Academy, Los Angeles, 2019).

Self Realization in Kashmir Shaivism, The Oral Teachings of Swami Lakshmanjoo, ed. John Hughes (State University of New York Press, Albany, 1995).

Shiva Sutras, The Supreme Awakening, ed. John Hughes (Lakshmanjoo Academy Book Series, Los Angeles, 2015).

Stava Cintāmaṇi of Bhaṭṭanārāyaṇa, ed. John Hughes (Lakshmanjoo Academy Book Series, Los Angeles, 2018).

The Mystery of Vibrationless Vibration in Kashmir Shaivism, Vasugupta's *Spanda Kārikā* and Kṣemarāja's *Spanda Sandoha*, ed. John Hughes (Lakshmanjoo Academy, Los Angeles, 2016).

Vijñāna Bhairava, The Manual for Self Realization, ed. John Hughes (Lakshmanjoo Academy Book Series, Los Angeles, 2015).

Unpublished texts from the Lakshmanjoo Academy (LJA) archive:

Bhagavad Gītārtha Saṁgraha of Abhinavagupta, translation and commentary by Swami Lakshmanjoo (original audio recording, LJA archive, Los Angeles, 1978).

Interview on Kashmir Shaivism, Swami Lakshmanjoo with Scholars and John Hughes (original audio recordings, LJA archive, Los Angeles 1980).

Janmamaraṇavicāragranthaḥ, *Janma Maraṇa Vicāra of Bhaṭṭa Vāmadeva*, Swami Lakshmanjoo (original audio recording, LJA archive, Los Angeles, 1980).

Parātrīśikā Laghuvṛtti, with the commentary of Abhinavagupta, translation and commentary by Swami Lakshmanjoo (original audio recording, LJA archive, Los Angeles, 1982).

Parātrīśikā Vivaraṇa, with the commentary of Abhinavagupta, translation and commentary by Swami Lakshmanjoo (original audio recording, LJA archive, Los Angeles, 1982-85).

Shri Kramanaya Pradīpikā – Shining Light on the Twelve Kālīs, by Swami Lakshmanjoo (Hindi), 1958. English translation by Pranath Kaul, 2003 (LJA archive).

The Tantrāloka of Abhinavagupta, Chapters 5 to 18, translation and commentary by Swami Lakshmanjoo (original audio recording, LJA archive, Los Angeles, 1972-1981).

Vātūlanātha Sūtras of Anantaśaktipāda, translation and commentary by Swami Lakshmanjoo (original audio recordings, LJA archive, Los Angeles, 1979).

Index

A
Abhinavagupta 23, 28, 34, 41, 47, 55, 62, 64, 65, 71, 76, 77, 78, 84, 89, 99, 103, 104, 105, 108, 154, 164
Abhiṣeka 23
Absorbed 53, 58, 104, 155
Achievement 5, 54
Actor 82
Adharma 67
Āgama 75, 76, 77
Aghora 42
Agni 42
Aiśvarya 67
Ajña 5
Ajñāna 68, 77
Alert 2, 52, 54
Alertness 53, 54
Amṛta 97
Amṛteśvara 115, 140
Anaiśvarya 67
Anaiśvarya 68
Ānanda 14, 77, 81, 82, 93, 107, 160
Anantabhaṭṭāraka 45
Āṇavopāya 69, 86, 87, 88, 98, 99, 102, 105, 107
Ancient 24, 66
Aṅga 94
Anugraha 13, 27, 89, 95
Anupāya 86, 87, 88, 89, 90, 94, 95, 99, 100, 101, 102, 105, 106, 107
Anuttara 107, 149, 150
Apāna 43, 142, 159
Āpara 15
Appearances 110, 152
Ascetic 83, 85
Aspirant 25, 33, 51, 60, 94, 99, 164
Astray 22, 54
Asvatantra 5, 113
Ātma 10, 98
Attentive 39, 58
Automatic 1, 2, 23, 40, 52, 53, 58, 59, 62
Automatically 6, 52, 53, 59
Awakened 99, 152, 156
Aware 54
Awareness 7, 53, 54, 58, 79, 142, 152, 160
B
Balance 10, 11
Balled 52, 53
Balling 52
Bhairava 9, 34, 35, 36, 37, 38, 39, 40, 41, 42, 47, 67, 73, 74, 103, 154, 155, 156, 157, 158, 162, 163
Bhairavī 34, 160
Bhakti 20
Bheda 11, 12, 13, 16, 18, 91, 150
Bhoga 50, 103, 110
Bhogaṁ 50
Bhūcarī 39, 40
Bhujaṅgavat 87
Bhuvanādhva 16, 17
Binding 87
Bindings 77
Birth 96, 150, 153
Bliss 2, 14, 59, 77, 80, 96, 107, 151, 156
Blissful 101, 103, 118, 141, 151, 159, 160
Bodha 109
Bondage 77, 150, 155
Bored 61
Boring 61
Brahma 4, 5, 10, 62, 64, 120
Brahmāṇḍa 53
Breath 1, 4, 6, 7, 43, 51, 52, 62, 69, 106, 142, 158, 159
Breathe 4, 51, 52, 102
Breathing 4, 51, 52, 53, 90, 106
Breaths 1, 6, 43, 51, 52, 53, 69, 70
Buddhi 59, 67, 68, 91, 160
Buddhibedha 68
C
Cakrodāya 102
Candra 52, 74
Cidrasa 9
Cit 9, 14, 15, 77, 81, 82, 93, 107
Citi 80
Cittā 103
Coagulated 9, 10
Coagulation 9
Cobra 87
Cognition 40, 42, 86, 103, 145, 148
Cognitive 39, 42, 148
Conceal 45
Concealing 13, 42, 82
Conceals 42
Concentration 10, 58, 149
Conquer 85, 94
Contemplation 2, 50, 149
Creation 13, 14, 15, 17, 42, 44,

63, 78, 82, 141, 148
Creative 44
Creator 17, 112
Crookedness 26
Crux 8
Cure 36
D
Dakṣine 117, 118, 140
Dances 118, 157
Dancing 20
Darśanas 26
Death 38, 39, 50, 109, 110, 116, 117, 118, 143, 150, 155, 156
Deaths 5, 49, 108
Depression 101, 152
Desire 51, 53
Destroyer 38, 142, 145
Destruction 13, 14, 15, 42, 82, 143, 144, 148
Detachment 29, 67
Devotion 20, 32, 52, 53, 111, 116, 154, 155, 156, 160
Dhāraṇa 35
Dharma 20, 67, 68, 82
Dhyāna 2
Differentiated 9, 18, 150, 152
Dikcarī 39, 40
Dīkṣā 23, 50
Disaster 37
Discipline 32, 94
Diseases 49, 50
Disqualification 26
Doer 112, 113
Doubt 24, 34, 89
Doubts 98, 99, 152, 159
Dreaming 11, 67
Dreamless 11
Dualistic 74, 82
Duḥkha 5, 60, 155
E
Ecstasy 7, 54, 96, 104
Effort 64
Ego 28, 29, 31, 50, 144, 145, 161
Ekāgra 57, 58, 59, 64, 71
Ekavīrā 46, 47, 128
Enemy 62, 67
Energies 14, 15, 16, 36, 39, 40, 77, 92, 93, 146, 148
Energy 11, 14, 15, 23, 35, 36, 77, 86, 96, 107, 143, 147, 154, 155, 160
Enjoyment 50
Enlighten 103
Entanglements 77
Exhale 52
Existence 3, 38, 80, 82, 116, 147, 152, 154, 155, 156, 157
Experience 8, 9, 26, 37, 45, 53, 55, 60, 61, 63, 80, 89, 101, 104, 111, 150, 153, 156, 160
Eyebrows 7, 51, 52, 58
Eyelash 116
F
Fasting 90
Fear 37, 45, 49, 50, 155
Fever 31, 155
Fierce 116
Fool 30
Forgetfulness 67
Fountain 80
Freedom 15
Fullness 7, 11, 13, 35, 45, 59, 63, 77, 99, 100, 104, 152
Furious 7, 84, 115, 116
G
Gaṇeśa 106, 158
Gap 32, 36, 63
Gītā 56, 62, 91
Glamour 3, 7, 13, 14, 104, 107
Glance 48, 87, 116, 117
Goddess 7, 116, 118, 142, 143, 147, 160, 161, 162, 163
Gods 5, 10, 11, 39, 145, 158, 162, 164
Grace 19, 23, 27, 37, 80, 89, 95, 99, 154, 156
Grammar 26, 41
Gratitude 104
Greatest 16, 31, 37
Greatness 102, 111, 153
Guru 87, 97, 99
H
Haṁsa 43
Hanumān 106
Happiness 54, 141
Hate 50
Heart 37, 51, 52, 96, 99, 100, 157, 159, 160, 161, 162, 163
Heaven 5, 6, 44, 97
Hell 6, 110, 111, 112
Highest 16, 46, 54, 100, 101, 102, 147, 149
Holiness 1
Hope 50, 51, 80
Hṛdaya 99, 162
Human 57, 82, 114

Husband 20, 32, 33, 34
Hypocrisy 7
I
Icchā 15, 77, 81, 82, 93, 107
Ignorance 3, 23, 24, 40, 62, 67, 68, 70, 73, 77, 82, 97, 99
Illusion 9, 15, 18, 24, 150, 152, 153
Imagination 114, 153
Immortal 47, 156
Impurities 62, 63, 98
Independence 11, 96, 112
Individuality 5, 83
Indriya 92, 159
Inhale 52
Initiation 22, 23, 24, 27, 87, 95, 99
Instantaneously 48
Intellect 59, 67, 68, 160
Intoxicate 54
Introverted 79, 80, 93
Īśvara 6, 12, 13, 15, 44, 45
Īśvaraprerito 5, 120
J
Jag 7
Jāgrat 11, 12, 67, 68
Japa 90
Jīva 83, 93
Jñāna 15, 20, 28, 67, 68, 77, 81, 82, 86, 93, 107
Jñānendriya 39
Journey 77, 102
Joy 47, 53, 54, 59, 60, 61, 62, 101, 104, 111, 112, 151
K
Kalā 16, 17, 46
Kāla 116, 144
Kāla 38, 117
Kalādhva 16, 17
Kalāpa 108, 145
Kālasaṁkarṣinī 7, 117
Kālī 115, 116, 117, 118, 140
Kālīs 14, 15, 140, 148
Kalpita 23, 24
Kāṇāda 83, 84, 85
Kāraṇam 41, 42, 127
Kārikās 55
Karma 50, 109, 110, 112, 138, 155, 156
Karmendriya 39
Kartā 44, 113
Khecarī 39, 40
Kingdom 33, 40, 70, 80, 106, 115, 116, 148
Kleśaḥ 85, 133
Knowledge 14, 15, 20, 27, 29, 67, 73, 77, 79, 81, 86, 101, 156
Krama 23, 140
Kriyā 15, 77, 81, 82, 93, 107
Kṣemarāja 55
Kṣipta 57
L
Lakṣaṇam 2, 75, 119
Liberation 75, 150
Limitation 34, 35, 40, 81, 100, 143
Limitations 77
Limited 75, 80, 81, 82, 93, 101
Limiting 74
Liṅga 75
Love 32, 48, 52, 53, 54, 84
M
Madhyanāḍī 7, 43
Mahābhairava 34
Mahābhairavī 34
Mahākāla 117, 146
Mahākālī 115, 116
Mahāmāyā 44, 45
Maheśvara 12
Mahograkālī 115
Malas 62
Manifest 97
Manifestation 9, 77, 79, 83, 87, 97
Manifested 14, 15, 77, 97, 153
Mankind 97
Mantra 12, 20, 44, 45, 90, 92, 93, 95
Mantreśa 12
Mantreśvara 12
Mārga 51
Mārgeṇa 51
Māyā 15, 18, 29, 44, 45, 97
Meaning 2, 17, 18, 43, 45, 47, 57, 65, 72, 79, 88, 93, 109
Meaningless 72
Means 3, 4, 5, 6, 9, 10, 11, 12, 13, 16, 17, 23, 25, 26, 27, 29, 31, 32, 33, 34, 37, 38, 39, 40, 41, 43, 44, 45, 46, 47, 48, 51, 52, 53, 54, 57, 59, 60, 62, 63, 64, 65, 66, 67, 68, 70, 71, 74, 77, 78, 79, 80, 82, 85, 86, 87, 88, 91, 92, 94, 97, 98, 99, 100, 101
Meditation 2, 7, 50, 58, 66, 83, 84, 90, 108, 109, 149, 155, 158
Memory 46, 81
Mercy 36
Mind 20, 23, 24, 27, 29, 31, 55, 57, 58, 59, 61, 62, 63, 64, 73, 75, 76, 77, 79,

80, 85, 86, 89, 92, 93, 94, 95, 98, 103, 104, 115, 143, 155, 156, 161
Misbehavior 27, 32
Mischievous 32, 110, 111
Mislead 30, 32
Misunderstanding 27, 91
Mokṣa 75, 76, 77, 78, 132
Money 10, 23, 29, 115
Monistic 74
Moon 42, 147, 151
Mother 33, 34, 116, 117, 147
Mūḍhaḥ 53, 54, 91, 135
Mudrā 90
Mukha 92, 93
Mūrti 74, 75
Mystery 45
N
Nāḍī 43, 69
Nakṣatra 38
Nature 15, 21, 25, 26, 28, 36, 37, 38, 40, 42, 59, 61, 62, 63, 78, 79, 81, 91, 92, 95, 96
Neglect 10
Nimeṣaṇa 67
Nirmala 3
Nirvikalpa 18, 81, 93, 102
Nivṛtti 17, 46
Nothingness 38, 116, 148
Nourishing 29, 61
Nyāya 26
O
Oath 56
Obey 56
Observers 104
Obstacle 72
Obstacles 64, 65, 71, 72, 73
Oneness 82, 150, 151, 156, 157
Opening 52
Openings 43
Organs 39, 40, 59, 92, 159
P
Padādhva 16, 18
Parā 14, 15, 117
Parabhairava 38
Parādevī 117, 118
Paramāṁ 116
Paramārtha 108, 109
Paramaśiva 34, 102
Parameśvara 65, 66, 83, 85, 88, 131
Parāparā 14, 15, 117, 118
Parāśakti 117
Parātītā 117, 118, 140
Parātrīṁśikā 16, 104
Pārvatī 106, 115, 160
Passive 62
Paśu 39
Paśyan 59
Paśyantī 93, 95
Pātāl 76
Patāñjalī 59
Path 17, 18, 45, 51, 72, 110, 150
Pati 32, 33, 34, 66, 67
Peace 50, 118, 157
Penance 83, 84, 157
Perceivers 12
Played 82
Player 82
Poison 87, 90
Pores 43
Posture 90
Postures 90
Potter 112, 113, 114
Powers 72
Prabho 65, 66, 131
Prabhoḥ 98, 136
Prabuddha 54
Practice 24, 52, 55, 58, 59, 64, 76, 90, 94, 106, 149
Prajñā 101
Prakāraiḥ 19, 20, 123
Prakāśa 42, 46, 47, 69, 79, 147
Prakaṭaḥ 37, 38, 127
Prakaṭībhūtaṁ 37, 126
Pralayākala 12
Pramāṇa 46, 69, 148
Pramātās 45
Pramātṛ 12, 42, 44, 46, 148
Prameya 46, 69, 148
Pramiti 42, 46
Prāṇa 1, 43, 142, 158
Pratyabhijñā 7, 65, 92, 93
Pratyabhijñāhṛdaya 79
Problem 30, 84
Problems 71
Prohibited 52
Protection 13, 14, 15, 33, 42, 82, 148
Pṛthvī 102
Pūja 90, 91, 115, 140, 159
Punishment 19, 20, 28, 32, 110
Purity 21
Pūrṇānanda 96

Q
Qualification 24
Qualifications 24, 34, 35
R
Rāma 65, 66, 67, 68, 69, 70, 72, 73, 74, 96, 97, 100
Rāmacandra 96, 97
Rāmāyaṇa 95
Rasa 9, 90, 141
Real 8, 10, 18, 29, 73, 74, 79, 81, 82, 84, 113, 114, 116, 148, 153 156, 160
Reality 7, 10, 20, 21, 41, 61, 79, 81, 88, 91, 96, 102, 105, 147, 150, 152, 153, 170
Realization 29, 78, 99, 154, 156
Recitation 55, 90, 119, 149, 158
Recognition 7, 92
Reflection 90, 91, 155
Refuge 10, 36, 111, 112, 116, 117, 159
Relief 36, 71, 72
Remembrance 47, 157
Romakūpa 43
Ṛṣi 83, 85
Ṛtaṁ 59
Rudra 5
S
Sadāśiva 12, 13, 15, 44, 45, 115, 116
Sādhaka 51, 57, 60, 164
Sādhana 55
Sadness 60, 104
Sahasraṁ 64, 65
Sakala 12, 13
Śakti 11, 14, 15, 35, 40, 67, 77, 81, 82, 84, 85, 92, 93, 96, 107, 117, 155
Śaktipāta 26, 37, 99
Śaktis 14, 39, 40, 77, 84, 85, 92, 93
Śāktopāya 15, 86, 87, 88, 98, 99, 100, 102, 105, 107
Samādhi 54, 56, 58, 90
Samāna 43
Śāmbhavopāya 86, 87, 88, 98, 99, 100, 101, 102, 105, 106, 107
Saṁhāra 13, 143, 148
Saṁkalpa 108, 109
Śāṁkarīṁ 22, 123
Saṁkarṣinī 117, 118, 140
Saṁsāra 3, 5, 9, 10, 24, 32, 35, 36, 37, 40, 97, 108, 109, 126, 158
Saṁvid 81, 157
Śāntā 17, 46
Śāntātītā 17, 46
Sarvajño 31, 125
Satisfaction 36
Savikalpa 19
Search 10, 62, 75, 159
Searching 1
Service 23
Sevayā 23
Sex 39, 40
Sexual 40
Shrunken 39
Sign 48
Simultaneous 21
Simultaneously 21
Sinful 110, 111
Śiṣya 97, 115
Śiva 5, 12, 13, 14, 15, 16, 18, 20, 26, 29, 32, 33, 34, 35, 36, 37, 44, 45, 46, 63, 65, 66, 67, 71, 73, 74, 75, 82, 83, 84, 90, 93, 96, 99, 106, 107, 111, 112, 113, 114, 115, 118, 154, 155, 156, 157, 159, 160, 161
Śivadṛṣṭi 71, 104
Sleep 2, 12, 54
Smell 40, 163
Smṛti 46
Somānanda 71, 73
Sorrows 60
Soul 49, 50, 96, 97, 101, 116, 154
Sound 18, 94
Spanda 51, 53, 55,
Speaker 17, 18, 36
Spirituality 28, 29, 31
Sṛṣṭi 148
State 1, 11, 12, 15, 19, 42, 44, 45, 51, 53, 54, 56, 57, 58, 60, 61, 63, 64, 66, 67, 68, 70, 71, 73, 76, 79, 80, 81, 82, 83, 86, 87, 90, 91, 92, 94, 95, 101, 102, 104, 105, 107, 147, 148, 149, 150, 151, 152
Sthiti 13, 148
Subjective 2, 17, 42, 62, 141, 142, 148
Subjectivity 12, 92, 148
Śuddhavidyā 12, 13, 15, 44, 45
Suffer 110
Sufferings 110, 158
Sukha 5, 59
Superior 44
Supreme 1, 11, 18 14, 34, 35, 42, 49, 50, 51, 63, 64, 65, 90, 91, 99, 107, 147, 149, 150, 151, 154, 156
Suṣumnā 7
Suṣupta 11

Svacchanda 42, 90
Svacchandabhairavam 41, 127
Svacchandanātha 42, 44, 45, 46, 47
Svapna 11, 67, 68, 152
Śvarga 6
Svarūpa 78, 79, 80, 81, 82, 95, 96
Śvāsāt 98, 99
Svatantra 90
Svātantrya 11, 14, 15, 82, 87, 88, 89, 96, 106, 112
T
Tantra 65, 78, 100
Tantrāloka 15, 28, 34, 41, 55, 65, 73, 78, 88, 89, 100, 111, 171
Taste 9, 26, 30, 40, 53, 61, 89, 90
Tattva 16, 17, 21, 38, 163
Technique 70
Temper 28
Tirodhāna 13
Topmost 31
Torture 36, 37, 48, 60, 115
Touch 84, 87, 92, 99, 106, 118, 159, 162
Tragedy 48, 111
Transcendental 9, 148
Treasure 11, 151, 162
Trident 117
Trika 75, 76, 77, 83, 85, 148
Triśula 117
Turya 1, 11, 13, 14, 15, 56, 147, 148
Turyātīta 11
Tuṣyati 57, 59, 130
U
Unaware 58
Underworld 76
Universal 4, 42, 48, 49, 69, 70, 74, 75, 151, 153
Unlimited 81, 144
Unparalleled 59, 107
Upāya 99, 102, 106, 107
Upāyas 88, 98, 99, 101, 102, 104, 105
Utkrānti 50
Utpaladeva 71, 93, 170
V
Vācaka 17
Vācakādhva 17, 18
Vācya 17
Vācyādhva 17
Vairagya 67, 68
Vaiśeśika 26
Vāmadeva 42
Vasiṣṭha 76, 97, 100
Vasugupta 55
Vāyu 4, 162
Veda 25
Vedānta 26, 75, 76, 94
Vein 6, 7, 43, 52, 53, 69
Veins 43
Vidyā 17, 46
Vijñānākala 12, 13, 44, 45
Vikalpas 76, 77, 81, 161
Vikṣipta 57, 58
Vimala 109
Viṣṇu 5, 10
Viśvaṁ 35, 126, 144, 159
Viśvātma 42
Vow 57
Vrata 90, 157
Vṛtti 40, 77, 92, 93, 104
Vyāna 43
W
Wakefulness 11, 12, 67
Watchfulness 59
Weakness 67
Worldly 3, 19, 20, 27, 29, 50, 60, 100, 104, 145, 155, 157
Worship 90, 106, 155, 164
Wrath 115
Y
Yoga 4, 20, 57, 58, 59, 60, 90, 120
Yoga 20, 56, 57, 59, 76, 97
Yogi 4, 52, 56, 61, 62, 63, 64, 66, 86, 87, 91, 101
Yogic 69, 70, 72, 90
Youth 50, 110, 111
Yukti 98, 99

Lakshmanjoo ACADEMY

The teachings of Swami Lakshmanjoo are a response to the urgent need of our time: the transformation of consciousness and the evolution of a more enlightened humanity.

The Universal Shaiva Fellowship was established under Swamiji's direct inspiration, for the purpose of realizing Swamiji's vision of making Kashmir Shaivism available to the whole world. It was Swamiji's wish that his teachings be made available without the restriction of caste, creed, color or gender.

The Universal Shaiva Fellowship and the Lakshmanjoo Academy, along with the Kashmir Shaiva Institute (Ishwar Ashram Trust), India, have preserved Swamiji's original teachings and are progressively making these teachings available in book, audio and video formats.

This knowledge is extremely valuable and uplifting for all of humankind. It offers humanity a clear and certain vision in a time of uncertainty. It shows us the way home and gives us the means for the attainment of complete Self-Realization.

For information on Kashmir Shaivism or to support the work of The Universal Shaiva Fellowship and the Lakshmanjoo Academy and Kashmir Shaiva Institute (Ishwar Ashram Trust) visit the Lakshmanjoo Academy website or email us at info@LakshmanjooAcademy.org.

www.UniversalShaivaFellowship.org
www.LakshmanjooAcademy.org
www.IshwarAshramTrust.com

Instructions to download audio files

1. Go to https://www.lakshmanjooacademy.org/wisdom4-443
   code: WisdomKS

2. Fill out the email opt-in form to add your name
   to the Lakshmanjoo Academy email list.

3. When you click the button in the follow-up email
   to confirm your email subscription you will be
   directed to the audio page for your purchase.

   If you have any difficulties please contact us at:
   https://www.lakshmanjooacademy.org/contact

The streaming video of the lectures is also available for purchase and can be found on our website https://www.lakshmanjooacademy.org/purchase-video-series-wisdom-of-kashmir-shaivism

www.ingramcontent.com/pod-product-compliance
Lightning Source LLC
Chambersburg PA
CBHW070139080526
44586CB00015B/1767
* 9 7 8 1 9 4 7 2 4 1 2 1 3 *